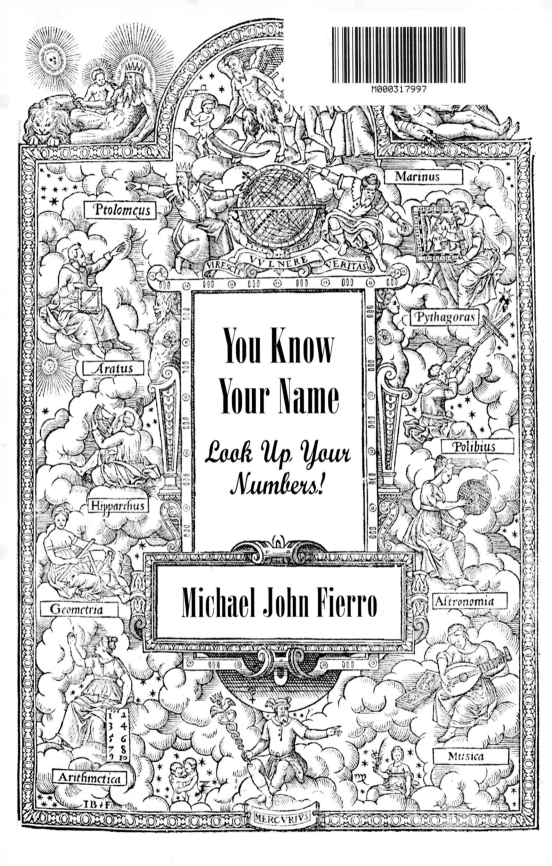

You Know
Your Name
Look Up Your Numbers!

Michael John Fierro

YOU KNOW YOUR NAME...
LOOK UP YOUR NUMBERS!
Michael John Fierro

Design
Gregg Hinlicky

Cover Art
Gregg Hinlicky with an assist by Raffaello Sanzio da Urbino

Printed in the United States

First Edition
July 2010

Published by:
Aerodale Press
Post Office Box 1521
Toms River, NJ 08754
www.aerodalepress.com

ISBN 978-1-4507-2282-7

TABLE OF CONTENTS

Introduction

We live in a world that is influenced, controlled, and ruled by numbers. In our conscious selves we may be totally unaware of the influence of these numbers. But at all times the vibrational energy of numbers is at work. It is this "influence of numbers" that is the basis for numerology.

As conscious, ego-driven human entities, we pay attention to and follow the signposts and symbols, which surround us at every turn. Street signs, warning signs, weather reports and stock reports, are all examples of indicators to which we listen and by which we are influenced. These are signs which we have been instructed to listen to and obey. Yet within each and every one of us lies a series of symbols and signs, which will enable us to follow our true direction. No one need look any further than our own birth certificate (that imprint upon paper which is filled out and filed on the occasion of our birth) to find the ultimate help in self-understanding and life direction. Just as a new vehicle comes equipped with an owner's manual, so too do we, as viable souls incarnated on this planet, come equipped with a manual. An instruction book. A means to understand and facilitate our individual destiny and fulfill our chosen purpose here on Earth.

Are we speaking of magic? Some hidden psychic gift, which only a handful of special privileged people possess? No....we are speaking about numerology, the ancient esoteric science of number interpretation. The science, which predates the birth of Christ, as discovered and developed by the ancient Chaldeans and by Pythagoras, the ancient Greek mystic and scholar. In a world where Pythagorean theories of mathematics and geometry, along with the musical scale as we currently know it, are accepted and taught in the educational systems, isn't it a little ironic that his other study and passion is not even mentioned or acknowledged? I find it hard to believe that the modern educational systems accept one part of a man's teachings, while not even giving recognition to another.

Within these pages, I wish to introduce you to yourself. More specifically, a means for you to introduce yourself to self. I wish to hand you the key with which you may unlock the treasure chest of true understanding, thus enabling you to follow your path toward true growth and enlightenment. The way for you to manifest as your chosen vibration to create SELF, so that you, as an individual part of the collective whole may assist in the journey of all back to the Great Spirit from which we all sprang forth. Through each of us living our individual vibration, will the whole be best able to re-form as true spirit.

Enjoy this gift, and the joy and enlightenment that will be revealed to each and every one of you. This information may be used in making decisions that influence the way you lead your life, and the path in life that you choose to follow.

Numerology helps explain the journey of the soul through the manifestation of the workings of the mind and the expression of the body. Back to it's original form, in a more enlightened and fulfilled fashion. An explanation of the *religio*, the journey that curves back within itself.

1

INTRODUCTION
TO NUMEROLOGY

CHAPTER ONE

INTRODUCTION TO NUMEROLOGY

"Mathematics is the study of numbers.
Numerology is the interpretation of numbers."

Numbers play an extremely important role in our daily lives. Whereas, mathematics is the calculation and study of numbers, numerology is the interpretation of numbers. Numerology is one of the most ancient of the esoteric sciences, and in some ways is a sister science to astrology. But, unlike astrology, it has never been mainstreamed. Astrology can, and will be affected by the discovery of any new planet in our solar system. There is absolutely no chance that anyone will discover a new number between 1 and 9. Numerology's beginnings date back to the time of the ancient Chaldeans and ancient Greece, approximately 500 B.C. Pythagoras, who may be better known for his mathematical theories, particularly the Pythagorean Theorem of triangles, is generally considered the "Father of Numerology". In ancient times, the political, spiritual, and religious leaders in their decision-making processes used the study of numerology.

Numerology, the clarion call of the only true vibration there is in the Universe. It is the rhythm and harmony of the cosmos. We are all a part of the melody, which is God's song. We are all a note in the symphony of all there is. Our being is in existence so we may play our particular note in this grand opera, which IS. Presented within these pages is a means for you to listen to the conductor (inner self) and follow it's direction. This will allow you to experience the joy of playing your own unique individual part, a part that can be heard, felt, and appreciated by everyone. This leads you to the point of being able to experience yourself as a part of the greater harmonious whole.

Numerology presents a way of understanding. It is a way of manifesting an understanding in all that you are and do. Through understanding where your spirit desires to go and directing your mind in the right direction, you are able to fully express yourself (the body) along the glorious path that you chose to travel. It is a system that is used to analyze and understand the forces, energies, and vibrations at work in an individual's life. In this fashion, it's use has not changed throughout the centuries. All the information necessary to formulate and interpret an individual's numerology chart is gathered from a person's birth date and name, exactly as it is spelled on the birth certificate. Confirmation and baptismal names are not used. It is extremely important that the exact name and spelling of that name as it appears on the birth certificate is used, since this the vibration that your soul chose for this lifetime. Within your name and birth date are all the talents, abilities, personality traits, and lessons that are present and necessary for this incarnation of your soul. *To put it another way, your date of birth is "the road in life which you are traveling"*, and your name is *"the vehicle that you are driving"*. You cannot get off that road, because you are unable to change your birth date, but you can change your vehicle, because you have the ability to change your name.

My study and interpretation of numerology is based on the use of your birth name only, since this is the vibration that your soul chose before entering this plane. In my practice, I have done numerous reading where an individual has seldom or never used their birth name, and it has always been interesting for me to see how "out of touch" with themselves these people really were. This consequently led to lives which were lived in confusion and possessed with a feeling of a lack of being connected which led to a sense that something was wrong, an undercurrent that coursed beneath the surface of their life. I therefore feel that it is extremely important for anyone to take time to reacquaint themselves with their original energy. By understanding this vibration, will you be better able to understand yourself. An important point to remember is that your birth name energy is always at work underneath any name changes, and name changes do not always work in someone's best interest. A new name may provide a vibration, which works in either concert or conflict with the original name. Many name changes throughout a lifetime often cause a sense of *"not really knowing who you are"*. Many women will identify with a shift in vibration upon marrying, and taking on their husband's name. The last name, or the surname, of any individual carries the karma of the family that bears the name. By marrying and taking on the husband's name, the individual takes on some of that karma, creating a situation where you are not only working through what you chose with your name, but working through something that you are not equipped to handle, as it has nothing to do with you. Your own experience, or the experiences of those you know, will confirm this. It is for this reason that I suggest careful consideration before taking on the name of someone else, in addition to your own. I have counseled people where an arbitrarily chosen new name has wreaked havoc in their lives, creating dynamics of addictive or aberrant behavior. The caution here is to choose a name wisely, but above all else, get to know and understand who you are first, as revealed by your birth name.

It must be noted that before there were alphabets, numbers existed. Alphabets were developed from numerical systems. To this day, the Greek and Hebrew alphabets are also representative of their numbering systems, i.e., alpha is 1, beta is 2, and so on. Additionally, numbers are a constant in the universe. All things resonate to a numerical vibration. In science, the table of elements lists a number for each and every element known to man, e.g., Hydrogen is 1, Helium is 2, and so on. Because of this, all that exists, be it animal, vegetable, or mineral, animate or inanimate, can be reduced to a mathematical equation. The exploration of space and the universe is done using mathematical equations and calculations. Thus, we can understand the importance of numbers in all that surrounds us in the world in which we live. Numbers are the constant, the *"thread that runs through all there is"*. As above, so below, as within, so without.

We note the importance of numbers in our daily lives. Phone numbers, bank accounts, house numbers, social security numbers, credit card numbers, and the list goes on. All these numbers and combinations of numbers play important parts in our every day existence. Consequently, it would be virtually impossible to live without the integral part, which numbers play in our lives. Taking all of this into consideration makes it easy to understand how the study of numerology can assist you in better comprehending the power and energy of your name. Once you have learned and understood the meanings and characteristics of the individual numbers from one to nine, you will be prepared to use this information consciously, and better understand how numerology is at work whether or not you know it exists.

My interpretation of numerology centers more on the human condition with all its frailties and potentials. It is my desire and intent to lead you on a journey of self-exploration and empowerment, wherein you come to a deep understanding of your own individual Being. That part of the Great Spirit/God energy which dwells within everything that you are, and everything that is part of the Universe that you inhabit is the focus. Through understanding, acknowledging, and acceptance are you able to take control of your life. By taking responsibility for your life, you are able to move forward with love and grace, and you move out of the finger pointing blame game, which takes so much energy to participate in.

YOUR NAME IS WHAT HAPPENS THROUGH YOU ON THE PATH OF YOUR LIFE (YOUR BIRTH DATE).

Numbers...the language of the Universe.

Numerology...the means for you to better understand yourself and those around you.

To paraphrase the immortal words of John Lennon...
"You know your name, look up your numbers."

2

THE ALPHABET

CHAPTER TWO

THE ALPHABET

When constructing a chart, you use the alphabet as you were taught in school. The twenty-six letters are each assigned a numerical value of 1-9. The more you practice numerology, the easier it will be to remember the value of each letter. In the meantime, use this chart for referral:

1	2	3	4	5	6	7	8	9
A	B	C	D	E	F	G	H	I
J	K	L	M	N	O	P	Q	R
S	T	U	V	W	X	Y	Z	

This is the basis of numerology. The alphabet and the numbers 1-9. Out of this comes all you need to know. Once you understand the basic meanings of the numbers, you are prepared to use numerology for yourself and in the understanding of those around you.

The letters A,E,I,O,U are the vowels. These letters are the components of the Soul/Being number of your name. Y is also considered a vowel (if you remember from school, Y is sometimes a vowel and sometimes a consonant). In my work, I only use Y as a vowel. The presence of a Y in a name will cause a degree of duality in an individual's personality. In a situation, where you are unclear as to whether the Y is a vowel or a consonant in its particular usage, you should always look at someone's chart in two ways, one with the Y as a vowel, and one with the Y as a consonant. When doing a chart and reading on a person, it will become clear to you which position and interpretation is the more accurate. In a case where Y is the only vowel in a syllable, then it should be viewed as a vowel.

The remaining letters are the consonants, which make up the Image/Personality number of an individual's name. The hard shell which serves as the vessel, encasing the Soul/Spirit.

Pythagoras, the Father of Numerology

3

THE MEANINGS
OF THE NUMBERS

CHAPTER THREE

THE MEANINGS OF THE NUMBERS

In this chapter, you will learn the meanings of the individual numbers, 1-9, along with the meanings of what are known as the Master Numbers, which are 11, 22, 33, 44, and (in rare situations) 55. Each number has both positive and negative attributes assigned to it, and through understanding how these numbers interact with each other in a chart, will you begin to be able to interpret their meaning. I will introduce you to the attributes and the symbology of the numbers.

The individual numbers came about to solve the inherent problems of the preceding number, and by so doing, allow for the progression and cyclic nature of numbers.

1-9 = THE EXPERIENCES OF LIFE

DOUBLE NUMBERS = THE KNOWLEDGE OF LIFE

MASTER NUMBERS = THE WISDOM OF LIFE

Divine INTELLIGENCE directs EXPRESSION.
Divine LOVE unfolds our CONSCIOUSNESS.

BY GUIDING THE PROCESS, YOU CAN AFFECT THE OUTCOME!

0	1	2
The Universe/God (Higher power)	The Beginning	Polarity (light/dark)
3	4	5
Creation/Triangulation (the Word)	Form/Elements (structure)	Expansion/Balance (transition)
6	7	8
Responsibility (matter/carbon)	Knowing/Learning (science)	Power/Knowledge (material manifestation)
	9	
	All There Is (higher consciousness)	

ONE (1)

"In the beginning God created the heaven and the earth. And God called the light Day, and the darkness he called Night. And the evening and the morning were the first day."

-- Genesis 1:1, 5

The number ONE represents the qualities of individualization, self-expression, initiative, leadership, director, the ability to handle the main issues, responsibility. It has a great deal to do with an individual's sense of self, and how he/she may relate to self and others. It is the beginning of all there is. It is represented by the letters A, J, and S

QUALITIES AND CONDITIONS OF THE NUMBER 1

POSITIVE	NEGATIVE
Originality	Aggressive
Individual	Dominant
Creative thinker	Willful
Inventiveness	Impulsive
Will	Boastful
Determined	Know it all
Courageous	Cynical
Initiative	Contrary
Executive ability	Talkative
Energy	Egotistical
Forceful	Reticent
Leadership qualities	Lazy
Self-determined	Imitator
Independent	Dependent
Strong opinions	Unstable
Masculinity	Fearful
Progressive	Braggart
Ambitious	Stagnant
Pioneering	Stubborn
Active	Bossy
Optimistic	Indecisive
Honest	Arrogant
Loyal	Hostile
Action-oriented	Ill-willed
	Tyrannical
	Impatient

ONE encompasses the individual, all the potential, new beginnings, the first of everything, the pioneer, the virgin, it stands alone, usually in front, the beginner, the creator, the instigator. It is independent, original, progressive, and the champion of progressive ideas, leadership and business. As the ONE seeks to individuate, through its need to grow, it FRAGMENTS!! This condition is answered by:

TWO (2)

"..And God made the firmament, and divided the waters which were under the firmament from the waters which were above the firmament; and it was so. And God called the firmament Heaven. And the evening and the morning were the second day"

-- Genesis 1:7-8

The number TWO represents duality, love, society, companionship, working with others, harmony, peace, mediation, sincerity, spiritual qualities acquired through sensitiveness, it accumulates wisdom through exploration and interaction, opposition, the other side. Two is one of the gender specific numbers, representing the feminine energy.
It is represented by the letters B, K, and T.

QUALITIES AND CONDITIONS OF THE NUMBER 2

POSTIVE	NEGATIVE
Agreeable	Sly
Modest	Extremist
Loving	Vacillating
Of service	Apathetic
Femininity	Indifferent
Gentle	Shy
Harmonious	Meek
Adaptable	Over-sensitive
Charming	Spineless
Diplomatic	Doormat
Friendly	Sulking

QUALITIES AND CONDITIONS OF THE NUMBER 2 *Continued*

POSTIVE	NEGATIVE
Musical	Malcontent
Rhythmic	Slacker
Receptive	Careless
Cooperative	Over conscientious
Considerate	Self-conscious
Tactful	Timid
Persuasive	Fearful
Sincere	Over detailed
Gracious	Procrastinator
Cultural	Introverted
Spiritual	Impatient
Sensitive	Cowardly
Patient	Mischievous
Peacemaker	Hostile
Mediator	
Protective	
Humorous	

TWO encompasses balance, harmony, and cooperation. It provides the ability to hear the other side, and provides grace of movement for dance, athletics, and the like. It is the mediator, politician, and fair-minded appraiser. As the TWO begins to grow, it must begin to create. It must expand in order to grow. This is answered by, and leads to:

THREE (3)

"And the earth brought forth grass, and herb yielding seed after his kind, and the tree yielding fruit, whose seed was in itself, after his kind: and God saw that it was good."

– Genesis 1:11

The number THREE represents the qualities of creativity, communication, creative self-expression, emotional expression, words... written or spoken. It is the creative dreamer, the imagination. It adds the qualities of social skills, and is emotional and kind. It is the combination of one and two, and is the first manifestation of the body, mind, and spirit. THREE represents the "heart" side of life. THREE adds creative talent in music, art, and writing, and all aspects of life where creativity is used. It also adds the qualities of charm, grace, and humor. It is represented by the letters C, L, and U.

QUALITIES AND CONDITIONS OF THE NUMBER 3

POSITIVE	NEGATIVE
Imaginative	Trivial
Creative	Self-centered
Inspiring	Extravagant
Emotional	Exaggeration
Gifted with words *(written or spoken)*	Gossiper
Visionary	Selfish
Artistic	Talkative
Communicative	Scattered energy
Intuitive	Intolerant
Entertaining	Jealous
Charming	Lack of follow through
Optimistic	Hypocritical
Joyful	Lack of direction
Lover of pleasure	Moody
Social	Critical
Gracious	Unforgiving
Kind	Worrier
Good taste	Whiner
Free of worry	Vain
	Superficial
	Prideful
	Boastful

The THREE encompasses the creation and creativity, the art of communication, and words written and spoken. It is the ability to speak up, and speak one's heart and mind. It requires focus, lest it becomes too scattered. THREE needs order so that it may continue to grow and expand. This condition is solved by:

FOUR (4)

"And God said, Let there be lights in the firmament of the heaven to divide the day from the night; and let them be for signs, and for seasons, and for days, and years:"

— Genesis 1:14

FOUR is the principle of creation manifesting as the four elements (air, fire, earth, and water). It creates discipline, foundation, stability, order, and regularity. FOUR is the power to create and attain. It makes manifest the opportunities of the 1, 2, and 3. It is represented by the letters D, M, and V.

QUALITIES AND CONDITIONS OF THE NUMBER 4

POSITIVE	NEGATIVE
Practical	Lacking discipline
Of service	Narrow-minded
Patient	Repressed
Organized	Picayune
Devoted	Clumsy
Patriotic	Dogmatic
Conservative	Crude
Pragmatic	Brusque
Dignified	Restrictive
Economical	Rigid
Trustworthy	Stern
Durable	Dull
Loyal	Lacking imagination
Powers of concentration	Very serious
Methodical	Overly detailed

QUALITIES AND CONDITIONS OF THE NUMBER 4 *Continued*

POSTIVE	NEGATIVE
Manager	Anal retentive
Constructive	Contrary
Works well with hands	Stubborn
Good sense of values	Exacting
Scientific	Argumentative
Serious	Opinionated (Fixed)
Determined	Confused by change
Able to relate to facts	Lacking vision
Good foundation	Lacking adventure
Dutiful	Unyielding
Orderly	Immovable
	Inflexible
	Stiff
	Hateful
	Suppressive
	Looks to get even

FOUR is the structure, foundation, and organization, which are demanded by the Universe. Without FOUR we would have chaos. FOUR is the builder, the bedrock of what is. It is the four directions, the four winds, and the four elements. If not able to express and create, it can be very restricted and stagnant. This condition creates the need for the:

FIVE (5)

"And God blessed them, saying, Be fruitful and multiply, and fill the waters in the seas, and let fowl multiply in the earth. And the evening and the morning were the fifth day."

– Genesis 1: 22-23

The number FIVE is the middle number between 1 and 9, thus it represents the fulcrum on which all other numbers balance. Consequently FIVE is a representation of balance. It is the most commonly occurring number in a name and provides the qualities of adaptability, mobility, imagination, a sense of adventure and curiosity. FIVE is also a representation of the five human senses, so it will also provide an inclination towards indulgence in "pleasures of the senses" if shown in abundance. In ancient Greece, FIVE was the number of man and was a representation of the five elements of fire, water, air, earth and psyche. It is a representation of travel, change, and movement. It is represented by the letters E, N, and W.

QUALITIES AND CONDITIONS OF THE NUMBER 5

POSITIVE	NEGATIVE
Progressive	Restless
Resourceful	Nervous
Adventurous	Discontented
Versatile	Critical
Active	Moody
Energetic	Sharp tongued
Powers of investigation	Quick temper
Curiosity	Lacks follow through
Administrator	Dissatisfied
Promoter	Scattered energy
Innovator	Impatient
Freedom lover	Hasty
Quick thinker	Impulsive
Understanding	Lacks application
Clever	Overindulgent
Social	Sensual pleasures
Changeable	Irresponsible
Traveler	Careless
Good companion	Thoughtless
Sense of law & order	Inconsistent
Persuasive	Sensationalist
Good sales ability	Occasional bad taste
Risk taker	Perverted

QUALITIES AND CONDITIONS OF THE NUMBER 5 *Continued*

POSITIVE	NEGATIVE
Creative mentality	Tasteless
Creative healer	Fearful of change
In tune with life's essence	Unsympathetic
	Unbalanced

Too much freedom and adventure needs to be channeled into positive action. The restlessness will be cured by the appearance of:

SIX (6)

"And God blessed them, and God said unto them, Be fruitful, and multiply, and replenish the earth, and subdue it: and have dominion over the fish of the sea, and over the fowl of the air, and over every living thing that moveth upon the earth. And God saw every thing that he had made, and, behold, it was very good. And the evening and the morning were the sixth day."

— Genesis 1: 28, 31

The number SIX represents a sense of responsibility, the family, purpose, law, the cosmic parent. It also is indicative of the mother and the father, along with the teacher, health care worker, and counselor. SIX is the healer. It is an energy that strives to take care of others. There is a need to balance the desire to be of service to others with the demands and needs of the family and home. It is represented by the letters F, O, and X.

QUALITIES AND CONDITIONS OF THE NUMBER 6

POSITIVE	NEGATIVE
Loving	Anxious
Nurturing	Worrier
Home loving	Meddling
Responsible	Overly idealistic
Able to adjust	Interfering

QUALITIES AND CONDITIONS OF THE NUMBER 6 *Continued*

POSITIVE	NEGATIVE
Musical	Overly conventional
Sympathetic	Prideful
Understanding	Smug
Domestic	Despondent
Stable	Unwilling to serve
Poised	Cynical
Protective	Egotistical
Powers of healing	Suspicious
Firm	Jealous
Balanced	Duty bound
Idealistic	Takes on others' troubles
Conscientious	Self-righteous
Sense of justice	Obstinate
Of service to mankind	Outspoken
Teacher	Slow to make decisions
Counselor	Self-sacrificing
Artistic	Domineering
Humanitarian	Digs heels in
Unselfish	Unwilling to hear
Harmonious	opposing view
Good judgment	Careless
Self-realized	Nasty
Compliant	Domestic tyranny
	Opinionated
	Co-dependent
	Succumbs to flattery

The SIX lacks sensitivity to spirituality. It is too willing to accept life without exploring the deeper meaning to gain understanding. This lack of spirituality leads to the need for the:

SEVEN (7)

"So God blessed the seventh day and hallowed it, because on it God rested from all the work that he had done in creation."

-- Genesis 2:3

SEVEN represents the inner self, spirituality, the powers of analysis and understanding. It seeks to uncover the hidden facts and meanings of things. It is a number of religion, intuition, the mystic, the researcher, the teacher and writer. It has a strong interest in mathematics and science and in understanding the rhythm and make up of the world it lives in. Knowledge is necessary to build on intuition (if you are going to go on your feelings, it would be a good idea to know what it is you are feeling). SEVEN is represented by the letters G, P, and Y.

QUALITIES AND CONDITIONS OF THE NUMBER 7

POSITIVE	NEGATIVE
Analytical	Melancholy
Technical	Fault finding
Introspective	Sarcastic
Peaceful	Cold
Poised	Aloof
Scientific	Skeptical
Spiritual	Confused
Keeper of faith	Humiliated
Trusting	Nervous
Stoic	Erratic
Refined	Faithless
Wisdom	Turbulent
Silence	Addictive
Seeks answers	Deceitful
Powers of calculation	Thievery
Observant	Cheating

QUALITIES AND CONDITIONS OF THE NUMBER 7 *Continued*

POSITIVE	NEGATIVE
Inventor	Crafty
Writing ability	Isolationist
Perfectionist	Overly introverted
Meditative	Anti-social
Interest in the occult	Shrewd
Charming	Repressive
Intelligent	Suspicious
Lover of solitude	Cynical
Dignified	Argumentative
Studious	Lacking generosity
Mystical	Unreasonable
	Demanding
	Too analytical
	Humiliating
	Contentious
	Malicious
	Suppressive
	Unsettled

SEVEN may create superstition or secrecy that leads to a quest for knowledge, money, and material goods. This is answered by the:

EIGHT (8)

The number EIGHT represents power, authority, money, and material things. It is the ruler, the business leader, the executive. It is the most karmic of all the numbers. EIGHT on its' side represents Infinity. The Law of Return. The Karmic Law. What goes around, comes around. That which you put out into the Universe will be returned in kind. It is the other gender specific number, representing a strong masculine energy. It is also a single digit master number that demands leadership with discernment. EIGHT is represented by the letters H, Q, and Z.

QUALITIES AND CONDITIONS OF THE NUMBER 8

POSITIVE	NEGATIVE
Powerful	Tyrannical
Authoritative	Strains to attain
Efficient	Overly energetic
Supervisor	Overly ambitious
Executive	Tension
Director of business	Egotistical
Gains recognition	Repressive
Good character analysis	Demands recognition
Good judgment	Lacks humanitarianism
Organized and organizer	Money difficulties
Concerned with world affairs	Impatient
Strength	Forceful
Capable	Materialistic
Discriminating	Intolerant
Practical	Worrying
Thorough	Scheming
Dependable	Power hungry
Self-reliant	Careless
Self-control	Controlling
Power to succeed	Poor judgment
Masculinity	Bullying
Money maker	Abusive
Athletic	Vengeful, Oppressive
	Unjust, Cruel
	Unscrupulous, Biased
	Lacks humility
	Bigoted, Immoral

The EIGHT's representation of power and authority must be tempered with a compassion for all humankind. This brings about the need for:

NINE (9)

The NINE is a combination of all the numbers and represents the universal human. It involves the qualities of compassion, selflessness, philanthropy, and the moderation of power. NINE has the inherent ability to conceive that the one is a part of the all. Without the number NINE, humankind would destroy itself through its inability to conceive of all that there is. The number NINE is represented by the letters I and R.

QUALITIES AND CONDITIONS OF THE NUMBER 9

POSITIVE	NEGATIVE
Humanitarian	Selfish
Philanthropic	Overly emotional
Brotherhood	Egotistical
Charitable	Overly sentimental
Compassionate	Indiscreet
Artistic	Impractical
Magnetism	Fickle
Sympathetic	Aimless dreamer
Understanding	Immoral
Romantic	Vulgar
Generous	Bitter
Broad viewpoint	Morose
Selfless service	In love with self
Perfection	Impulsive
Ideals	Lack of blame
Forgiving	Changeable in love
Writing	Moody
Religion	Depressed
Big opportunities	Careless finances
Higher consciousness	Seeks an easy time
Capable of living by divine standards	Approval seeker
Attracts money	Bad habits

QUALITIES AND CONDITIONS OF THE NUMBER 9 *Continued*

POSITIVE	NEGATIVE
Abundance of talent	Unkind
Aware	Scornful
Successful	Stingy
Finisher	Unforgiving
Merciful	Inconsiderate

NINE has the capacity to encompass all the good and bad of all the numbers. It innately looks back and sees the "family", while looking forward and seeing the "new" one. It is all that was and all that will be again!

Pythagoras (right) in a mathematical competition with Boetius of Dacia

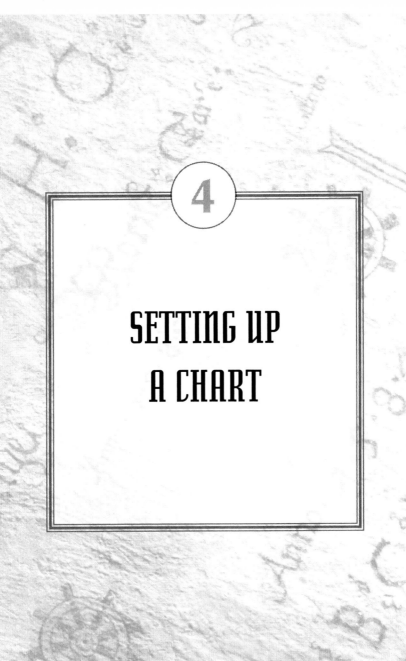

4

SETTING UP
A CHART

CHAPTER FOUR

SETTING UP A CHART

Now that you have an understanding of what the numbers mean, you can set up a numerology chart. In setting up a chart it is important to remember that you allow yourself enough room on your paper to do the appropriate calculations.

In my work, I only do charts on the name as it appears on the birth certificate. It is my belief that the name, which is imprinted upon that piece of paper, is the individual's "signature" in the Universe. I believe that prior to birth, the individual chooses the name that is to be given, and channels it through the parents. The reason for my belief is that the soul knows, coming into this existence, exactly what it must do, learn, and accomplish in this lifetime. All of this information is included in the spelling of the name and the birth date. You will be surprised at how accurately the chart on these types of names reflects the true character and personality of the person. It has been my experience that by doing the reading on the birth name, I am able to assist the individual in reconnecting with their true self.

IT IS VERY IMPORTANT THAT WHEN YOU DO A CHART, YOU USE THE EXACT SPELLING THAT APPEARS ON THE BIRTH CERTIFICATE, EVEN IF IT IS MISSPELLED. THIS ALSO HOLDS TRUE IN SITUATIONS WHERE THE NAME IS "BABY BOY/GIRL" JONES OR "FEMALE/MALE" SMITH.

What must be understood is the fact that any name, other than the birth name, is only a role that someone is playing in his or her own life. People who have had multiple name changes in their life can identify with a sense of confusion and disconnectedness within themselves. Women, the gender which society has dictated should change their name upon marriage, will also identify with a shift within when they marry and change their name. If you view name changes as a type of "Halloween costume" you will begin to understand what I mean. You are only playing the role of someone else, but underneath the "costume" is your true self, and when the costume is removed, you are still there. By doing charts on both the birth name, and any arbitrarily chosen name, and comparing the two, you will begin to discover the inner conflicts that an individual may be experiencing in their life. The more you do numerology, and the more charts you do, the more you will begin to understand this point. Do a chart on yourself, and if you have experienced a name change during the course of your life, see if you more closely identify with your birth name energy as opposed to the energy of the "new" name. My experience has shown me that many of the problems than an individual experiences during their life, come from a lack of understanding of who they truly are.

When setting up a numerology chart you will be looking at five major numbers. The first is the Soul Urge or Heart's Desire, the second is the Image or Personality number, the third is the Expression, the fourth is the Life Path or Birth Force, and finally you must take a good look at the Challenges, since these are the conditions which will prevent a person from fully living and experiencing their life to its fullest. The Soul Urge, Image, and Expression numbers come from the spelling of the name, while the Life Path and Challenge numbers are derived from the birth date.

In doing the calculations in numerology, it is important that the totals are reduced to a single digit for each name (the exception wold be if the number comes out as a master Number e.g. 11, 22, 33, etc.). In all instances Master Numbers are used in their double digit form. The single digit of each name (first, middle, last) should be added together to create another single digit.

In setting up the chart, write the name on a piece of paper, leaving enough room above and below the name to do the appropriate calculations. Your chart should look like this:

$$\underline{\quad 2 \qquad\qquad 17/8 \qquad\quad 8 \qquad\qquad\qquad 18 \;\;⑨}$$
$$1\;\;1 \qquad\quad 3\;\;\;59\;\;6\;1\;\;1\;\;=$$

BARACK HUSSEIN OBAMA

The numbers for the Soul Urge (the vowels) are placed above the name (the representation of the spirit or higher self). The numbers for the Image (the consonants) are placed below the name (the representation of the mind or lower self). The totals for each segment of the name are then placed above/below the number assignation. For example, the total of the vowels in Barack is 2. The total of the vowels in Hussein is 17, which becomes a single digit, 8, by adding the numbers of the double-digit 17 together. So, 17 becomes 1+7=8. The former digit and the new one are both shown, separated by a slash. Hence, Hussein = 17/8. Next you add the single digit totals of each name (2 + 8 + 8 = 18/9) to obtain the Soul Urge number, which is a 9. The total of the consonants in Barack is 16/7, Hussein is 15/6, and Obama is 6. Add the single digit (7 + 6 + 6 = 19/1) totals of each name and the image number is 1. Then you should add the single digit Soul Urge numbers to the single digit Image numbers to obtain the final number for calculating the Expression number. In this case, the 2 (Soul Urge) and the 7 (Image) of Barack equals a 9. The 8 (Soul Urge) and 6 (image) of Hussein equals an 14/5. The 8 (Soul Urge) of Obama and the 6 (Image) equals and 14/5. By then adding the 9 + 5 + 5 you obtain the expression number of 19/1. It is important to remember that you always reduce to a single digit in numerology, unless you end at a number, which is a master number, i.e., 11, 22, 33, 44, or 55.

In this sample chart, the soul urge is a 9, the Personality/image is a 1, and the expression is a 1.

SAMPLE WORKSHEET

This is an example of the format that you should use when constructing a chart. Again, be certain that you allow yourself enough room above, and below the name and birth date to do your calculations.

○ Soul Urge

△ Expression

□ Image

⇨ Life Path

The circle is where you would place the number of the vowels (the Soul Urge).
The square is where you would place the number of the consonants (the Personality/Image).
The triangle is where you would place the number of the total of the
Soul Urge and the Personality (the Expression).

Always remember to write out the birth date using the complete year, i.e., 1961.
Do not use the abbreviated version of a year, i.e., '61, as it is very important that
you include all the numbers in your calculations.

Underneath the birth date you will place the numbers of the challenges.

We live in a world that is influenced, controlled, and ruled by numbers.

5

WHO YOU
DESIRE TO BE

CHAPTER FIVE

THE SOUL URGE/HEART'S DESIRE
THE BEING/SPIRIT
WHO YOU DESIRE TO BE

Your soul knows what it has packed into the suitcase that is you...
and it knows what it has to go to the store (life) and buy!

"Now there are diversities of gifts, but the same Spirit. And there are differences of administrations, but the same Lord. And there are diversities of operations, but it is the same God which worketh all in all."

— I Corinthians 12:4-6

"For where your treasure is, there will your heart be also."

— Matthew 6:2

Your Soul needs the channel through which to flow, i.e., the Mind and Body. This is what you are here to manifest. This is your portion of the God energy. The desire and opportunity to experience all there is. Your soul's greatest creation would be to manifest that which your heart desires. Since this is what you want to be, you should pay heed to its calling. "Follow your heart", the old adage which has such great numerological basis. The function of the soul is to indicate its' desire…not impose it. It is your heart energy…home…a place of contentment and happiness…it is the birthplace of conception in your life…It is what you already are! *CONCEIVE.*

The Soul Urge is the inner self. It is who you would choose to be, were you given a magic wand and a wish to be or do anything you choose. It represents your inner desires, and is an indication of what would bring you the greatest joy and satisfaction in your life. Although, the Expression is who you must be in this lifetime, it would be prudent to take into consideration the vibration of the Soul Urge in making a decision as to how you are going to go about being that individual. In my experience and work with Numerology, I have many times found that an individual is doing one thing in his or her life, when in reality they yearn to be on another path, doing something else. When I question them about this and give them a "magic wand" to make a wish, they are often surprised by what they choose, but it does very closely resonate to the vibration of the Soul Urge. This is the place within you where you do "Conceive"; it is the place of inspiration and connection to the divine spirit. The Soul Urge is your best self, the unseen, but felt inner core. This energy affects your judgment, your outlook and the principles by which you live. It is the "prime motivator". This is the essential part of your inner being, that which you would most like to be. The Soul Urge is the motive behind the actions and the "why" of those actions. The following descriptions of the numbers in the Soul Urge position are a detailing of talents, abilities, and natural proclivities along with some of the negative tendencies. Use these descriptions to discern for yourself a career that will be the best outlet for these characteristics.

$$2 \qquad 17/8 \qquad 8 \qquad\qquad 18 \; (9)$$

$$1 \; 1 \qquad 3 \; 59 \; 6 \; 1 \; 1 \; =$$

BARACK HUSSEIN OBAMA

In the sample name, you would assign the appropriate number to each vowel, placing the number above the vowel. You then add the total of the vowels in each name always reducing to a single digit (unless the number becomes a Master Number of 11 or 22).

Barack, $1 + 1 = 2$; Hussein, $3 + 5 + 9 = 17/8$; Obama, $6 + 1 + 1 = 8$.
Then add the sums $(2 + 8 + 8 = 18/9)$

ONE is the creative, original and independent boss. ONEs like to tackle big issues and be in charge while doing so. More an employer than an employee, a ONE will thrive in a position that offers a leadership or management role. At times, the ONE may not be concerned with the details and they must be aware of their tendency towards being proud, and easily humiliated or embarrassed. The ONE is an active and driven individual with great ambition. They must guard against impatience and a critical nature as they may at times be unintentionally unkind. Their great drive and individualistic attitude may be self-centered and ego-driven. When balance is attained, the ONE is the person that others will look up to for leadership.

TWO is a sensitive and emotional energy that strives for peace and harmony. They are naturally diplomatic and often find themselves in a position of being a problem solver or mediator of others' disputes. The TWO is a thoughtful, loving, and devoted individual who works well with others. Not overly ambitious, the TWO may lack discipline. It is the energy of the worker who will dutifully follow the rules and orders of people in superior positions. The TWO naturally attracts things and may be a "good luck charm" of sorts. The TWO is tolerant, romantic and idealistic. This is an energy that is devoted, kind, helpful, easy-going, and mild-mannered. A natural helper who may be timid. TWOs are somewhat of a perfectionist. They love ease and comfort and are harmonious by nature. There is an innate appreciation and sense of beauty and grace that may manifest in a flowing, graceful style of movement. Shyness and easy embarrassment will often prevent the individual from fully expressing themselves through artistic or social activities.

THREE is a happy, optimistic and loving energy. It sets a good example for others and has an easy-going nature that laughs at bad times and lives with a happy-go-lucky, don't worry attitude. A THREE is emotional and loving and very much a social, creature who loves to play the role of host or entertainer. Threes love crowds and people, and they don't like to be alone. The THREE is artistic and creative and has innate abilities for writing, art, sculpture, music and similar endeavors. It appreciates things of beauty and has a discerning eye for that which spring from artistic or creative talent. The THREE has a sense of humor as well as a great interest in others. The ability exists to be a great communicator or public speaker. Being somewhat childlike, the THREE likes children and animals. It is vital and energetic and may view life as a game so it may not take it seriously. Threes are popular and the life of the party. They have great poise, confidence, and grace.

FOUR is the solid, conservative, and dependable individual who likes to serve. This is the energy of the military, police, government, or other organization where a strong sense of order and discipline is required. The FOUR likes the known as well as the conventional and traditional. They are punctual, detail oriented, thorough, faithful, constant, and loyal, as well as slow and steady. They may appear cold as the sense of discipline and decorum is a major facet of the energy. FOURs like peace, quiet, and stability. This is the father figure. Extremely practical, they tend to do what they are told. Cautious, slow, methodical, and organized they view the home as an institution. Talent may lie in the use of hands or with mechanical ability. The FOUR is honest with great integrity. They are also patriotic and the disciplinarian. Often they appear narrow-minded and inflexible in their approach to life.

FIVE is a lover of personal freedom who doesn't like to be tied down. They are easily bored and they thrive on activity, variety and being on the go. Travel, new people and new places are sources of interest and stimulation. FIVEs adapt quickly and they are fascinated by life and the adventure of life. Intellectual, curious, emotional, and changeable are all dominant characteristics of this number. A FIVE likes the outdoors, art, music, and science and generally is stimulated by people, places and things that provide pleasure. This individual doesn't like routine, restrictions, or waiting. They are spiritual in their own way, usually embracing unorthodox or different approaches to life and living. It is hard for them to take responsibility seriously and there is a tendency to easily let go of things. A FIVE is not bound by conventions or the ideas of others. This is an energy that adds spark to all in which they participate. The individual is attracted to, and greatly likes the opposite sex. Conversely, they are attractive to those around them. Love may be quick and deep and then the person moves on, breaking hearts in the process. The FIVE is the bohemian with a very strong individualistic streak. They want total personal freedom and often hold progressive and radical viewpoints. A love of speed, travel, different cultures and cuisines is paramount, as they appreciate food, the unusual, the strange and the unconventional. A FIVE is flexible and adaptable. They are self-starters who may begin many things, while not necessarily finishing them. This individual may be impatient but they are clever, intelligent, and resourceful with a seeming unending pool of great inner resources.

SIX is the number of the counselor, teacher, and healer. This is the "mother" energy that loves to give advice, manage others, and turn all wrongs into rights. Love, care and concern for others is a hallmark of this particular number. Family, home and friends are of the utmost importance. A SIX is a devoted, loyal friend. One who is kind, sympathetic, understanding, and generous with a broad-minded and conventional outlook on life. Doing for others is something that a SIX does willingly and with great gusto. This individual appreciates thanks and recognition and must be cautious that they allow reciprocal behavior to come their way. This number is best when working with others or with someone in need. It is artistic and loves beauty, music and comfort. With a SIX, everything is personal and they become easily involved emotionally. There is a great energy for healing, teaching, counseling and care-taking. Justice is another hallmark of this number. The SIX needs roots, and the stability of the home and family life allows it to blossom as they want to provide that for others. They willingly take on responsibility. This is the number of social conscience and is the humanitarian.

SEVEN is the thinker and the skeptic who questions all. SEVENs are known for not taking anything at face value. They are the ones who asks "why?" They love to gather information and are quite knowledgeable about many things. They embrace an intellectual and scientific approach to living. Math, science, research, teaching, and writing are pursuits in which the SEVEN is in its element. This number values silence, peace, and meditation. Spiritual, philosophical and intuitive a SEVEN has great inner wisdom and a very strong "quiet knowing". This person is highly attuned. The energy of the individual loves the country, nature, being alone. A busy, urban environment is not conducive to peace of mind for the SEVEN. While they enjoy being alone, they often fear loneliness. In occupational venues, the preference is to use the head over hands in work. This is the perfectionist. A SEVEN is shy and reserved and often appears aloof. They will reveal elements of self in their own time and on their own terms leading to them being often misunderstood. While being very emotional, those feelings are often hidden and they may be somewhat emotionally stunted. Conservative, wise, shy, stoic, taciturn, and calm are all characteristics. They love tradition and values and have an interest in that which is old. The SEVEN is extremely capable mentally.

EIGHT is the business minded worker or executive. This number shines when wheeling and dealing and often believes that bigger is better in business. An EIGHT takes charge and is a natural leader, often rising to high levels in management or an executive capacity. They are efficient, organized, a keen judge of people, an originator of sound ideas. and of what will be successful. Exacting, courageous, and determined are all qualities held by the EIGHT. An ambitious, hard work who loves money and success. An individual with great strength, imagination, and enthusiasm and EIGHT is dependable, trustworthy and honest. EIGHTs want achievement and are fearless, confident, self-assured when pursuing their goals. The EIGHT is at home in business and commerce and they may be quite magnanimous and philanthropic. This person loves the good fight, the dare, and the challenge to do and achieve where others have failed. With a goal in sight they have great drive.

NINE is the big brother, the universal man. They are understanding, thoughtful, sympathetic, and loving. A selfless person who loves people, they desire personal love, but belong to all. A NINE must learn to give to the all in order to receive personally. They are attractive, easily loved and give freely of self. This energy feels for others and wants to help. They are quite intuitive and know others' thoughts. The desire is to share with others. The NINE has a way with words and best teaches through personal example. They are quite spiritual and have great faith in the goodness of man. There exists an idealism and a need to know. The NINE is not materialistic and truly considers itself a member in good standing in the family of man. They want to do good for all. This is the helper, servant, and spiritual lover. One who is a dreamer and visionary. Altruistic, genuine, and sincere are additional qualities. They are artistic and love music, the arts and all that is cultural. It is imperative that the NINE exercises self-expression as this is how they make their mark in their world. Being tolerant and broad-minded, a NINE must be careful that they do not allow others to take advantage of them.

ELEVEN is the first of the Master Numbers. An ELEVEN may be a dreamer who is not practical. The great visions that are received must be made real if they are to do anyone good. This energy is idealistic and spiritual and believe they are tasked with saving the world. The ELEVEN likes to share ideas of god and religion but they must consider their fellow man in implementing ideas, as not everyone is ready to see as they do. This energy lives in another world and they must learn to balance the two worlds. They possess great inner strength and an inventive mind that must be put to use. Because of the special calling of the ELEVEN, they may not have many friends who are like minded. An ELEVEN is not materialistic as they exist more in the spiritual realm. It is important that this person follows their hunches and feelings. Learning to trust one's own intuition is paramount. They should associate more with people in general, and those who may be less fortunate in order to

increase their understanding and their ability to help. It is important
that the ELEVEN maintains faith to make manifest the world that is
envisioned. Often deeply religious they must learn to be with the public
and share knowledge freely.

TWENTY-TWO is the second Master Number and it has great
vision and imagination. They must develop the practicality to put it to
use moving away from the theoretical. They must be beneficial to others
and perfect that which they have come to teach. A TWENTY-TWO lives
in two worlds, but realizes they are not separate. They genuinely love
people and help wherever they can. This is a kind and patient leader
who is a master of any situation. This number calls on one to restore
harmony and order in your own way. This energy is spiritual and
progressive and works for improvement and enlightenment in the world.
The TWENTY-TWO is fair and trustworthy and holds beautiful ideals.
They must be steadfast and must not be swayed by others. It is important
to trust their own judgment and seek their own counsel. The guidance
received is true. As a Master Number, it is imperative that one does not
fail to follow the chosen path, while allowing others do the same.
Through this is gained appreciation. Also important is that the
TWENTY-TWO does not underestimate themselves. This is the master
builder who must build something worthy using down-to-earth pragmatism
and vision.

THIRTY-THREE is very rare in names. This is the highest
calling of Master Numbers that are possible in a name. The THIRTY-
THREE sees the divine order in things and is misunderstood by others
who do not have the vision. They must simplify their beliefs in order to
teach others. This energy sees harmony and good when others see
disharmony and evil. It perceives and loves the inner person and lives in

a world not understood by others. It is important to be a leader and teacher who leads by example, rather than preaching. Jealousy from others may be expected, although they may see the greater good in you. The THIRTY-THREE lives for others and the result is protection and provision. The goal is to teach others how to make the spiritual manifest in the material world. This number will have a following and must be willing to share the light. THIRTY-THREE is a master healer and is often associated with the Christ energy.

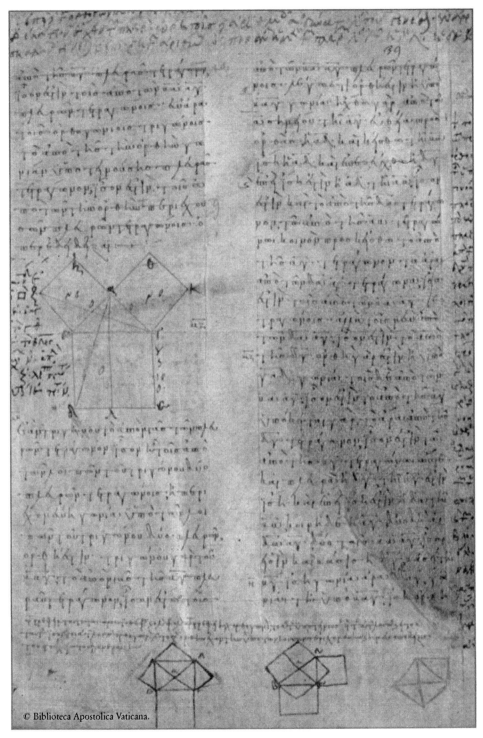

Vatican Copy of Euclid's "Elements" containting Pythagora's theorem

6

WHO YOU APPEAR TO BE

CHAPTER SIX

THE PERSONALITY/IMAGE–
THE DOING/MIND
WHO YOU APPEAR TO BE

IMAGE/PERSONALITY- This is your MIND. The "doing" energy of your existence. This is the tool (the vehicle) through which you have chosen to do the soul work. It is your "power tool". You must learn to understand and embrace this tool that you have chosen. You must realize that it is impossible to do the job of a saw when you are using, or think you are using, a hammer. This is your manifestation technique - that which you appear to be and that which you present to the people and Universe which surrounds you. Since this is what people will REACT to, it is important that you CREATE the best of what you are. "BE ALL THAT YOU CAN BE!" The function of the mind is to choose from its alternatives…the ego/mind, the physical body, or the spirit. This is "how others see you". It is the face you present to the world. This is the first impression number when you interact with others. The Image is the part of you that will immediately be "seen". It is the human condition/manifestation of the Soul Energy. This is the passive energy that you are when you are not in the state of acting or reacting. On one hand, in your quiet times, you will vibrate with the energy of this number. Conversely, the vibration of this number is that which will be seen and felt by those with whom you interact. The consonants that comprise the Image number are the shell that surrounds the Soul Urge.

It is important that the individual learns how to integrate this number with that of the Soul Urge. It is through this energy that your Soul Urge will manifest. The Personality/Image number combined with the Soul Urge creates the whole which is the Expression (explained in the next chapter). It is possible that the two numbers may have a degree of conflict or opposition between them. In these cases, one must learn to overcome the conflict and work towards a balance, to create a whole that is the harmonious sum of the parts.

BARACK HUSSEIN OBAMA

2 9 32 8	11 5	2 4		
16/7	15/6	6	=	19/$\boxed{1}$

In calculating the Personality/Image number, you place the appropriate number of each consonant underneath the letter. Then, you calculate the total of the consonants in each name. Barack, $2 + 9 + 3 + 2 = 16/7$; Hussein, $8 + 1 + 1 + 5 = 15/6$; Obama, $2 + 4 = 6$. Next, you take the single digit total from each name, and add them together: $7 + 6 + 6 = 19/1$

   ONE appears to be courageous and daring and often dreams of grand accomplishments. The ONE sees itself as the leader, the entrepreneur, and is also viewed as the instigator. Original in thought and appearance, this number is seen as a leader, manager or executive. This person is not one who likes to be told what to do. This is the individual that conceives and originates ideas, although it may not be inclined to finish that which is started. The ONE comes across in appearance as self-confident, self-assured and likable and may stand out in a crowd through demeanor or appearance. This individual must be aware of tendencies towards brashness, aggressiveness, being overbearing or too egocentric.

TWO is a number which envisions itself in a place of harmony and comfort. Love, companionship, family and friends surround this individual. There is a strong desire for harmonious and companionable surroundings. The TWO is a natural peacemaker or mediator and will have a tendency to attract others wishing a solution to disagreements or arguments. This person is seen as being diplomatic and fair-minded, as well as refined in language and appearance. The TWO has a strong desire to be liked. It is sensitive, caring and detail oriented. A good companion who is attractive, kind and gentle. This person is not a spotlight seeker and works well in the background and is usually a well-liked people pleaser, as well as a good listener. The TWO is somewhat shy and does not wish to attract attention to themselves. They usually present a neat, clean and orderly appearance. If negative, this individual may be lacking in self-confidence around others, while supersensitiveness will create strong surface emotions and a tendency to crying and being upset. In the worst case this number will exhibit sneakiness, shiftiness and being a liar.

THREE sees itself, and is seen as the social person. This person is popular while entertaining, creating, and being appreciated for their efforts. They like to be surrounded by beauty and art and are a center of joy and optimism. The THREE is the social center of attention while making sure that all are enjoying themselves. This person is creative in thought and action as well as being quick witted. The THREE is quite at home with an audience and will often be playful and childlike. This person must be aware of allowing the playfulness to interfere with work. A THREE is usually attractive, outgoing and popular with an infectious good attitude that affects all those who surround them. Creative and artistic in appearance, this person loves to talk and joke. On the negative side, they may be a gossiper and one who meddles in others' affairs. A negative THREE is also one who flaunts herself/himself and their sexuality. In the extreme, the negativity may be too serious and life will be burdensome. Often the THREE will be unable to deal with criticism or responsibility.

FOUR is seen as dependable and solid. This is the one whom others can turn to for protection. They have a strong sense of duty and service and are patriotic and willing to serve family, friends and country. Practical, orderly conservative, neat and clean cut in appearance and action, they are honest and reliable. A FOUR is willing to take on the task at hand to create the order, structure and discipline, which is an inherent part of the nature. This individual is self-reliant and will handle the tasks at hand, or delegate others to do that which must be done. If negative, they may appear stiff, rigid, and inflexible. There may be a tendency towards being a workaholic. The negative FOUR may be too cautious, while being anal retentive and restrictive. The truly negative FOUR will be rude and foul-mouthed.

FIVE is the free spirit looking for adventure. The FIVE has a great desire to travel and experience life along with new people, places and things. This person is seen as versatile, adaptable and willing to experience the new and different. A FIVE chafes at the tried and true and is constantly on the look-out for new adventures and experiences. This person demands and desires great freedom and is bored by routine. There will be great resistance to being restricted or tied down by people or circumstances.

True happiness with a partner comes when independence is offered and allowed. A FIVE is appealing to the opposite sex and may exude a level of sexuality. Part of their appeal is the sense that they are "game for anything" and they portray an appearance of willingness and inhibition. Somewhat bohemian in appearance and behavior, this is one who loves life and desires the freedom to experience it. A FIVE is attractive, popular, witty, funny and daring. This person is a good salesperson, who has a great ability to turn the abstract into the believable and concrete. The FIVE must beware of overindulging in pleasures of the senses as this is an easy tendency to fall into. Another behavior may be a tendency to repeat the same mistakes repeatedly until the appropriate lessons are learned. The FIVE must also be aware of a tendency towards risky or crazy behavior with a lack of caution.

SIX is the caretaker, attracting those with problems and circumstances that need tending. They are very domestic while be loving, compassionate, and kind. The SIX is willing to do for, and take care, of others. This person is the center of most circles, be it family, community, or work. The SIX takes great care in matters of home and garden. Issues of the home are paramount and they work to create an attractive, warm and loving environment. This individual is artistic, especially around the home. They love to create comfort and familiarity. The SIX is the responsible humanitarian who lives to take care of others, and heal everyone's "wounds". This person is a magnet for advice seekers and people in need of consoling. It is important to them that they feel appreciated and they must learn toestablish boundaries so their good and caring nature is not abused by others. In appearance, they exude a sense of comfort while also exhibiting the parent vibration. On the negative side, the SIX can be stubborn, opinionated, overbearing, smug and a busy-body. They must be aware of overindulging in comfort food. The SIX is often the person who rules the roost.

   SEVEN is the seeker who is forever looking for the answers to the questions that are asked and unasked. Their wisdom springs forth from a deep source and they have an unquenchable thirst for knowledge. A SEVEN appears distant and aloof to outsiders and many may consider them to be unapproachable. Oftentimes they are thought to be "stuck-up" This comes from being guarded, hiding their true feelings and emotions. There is an enigmatic, otherworldly quality that this person conveys. The SEVEN is analytical and the investigator who enjoys books, libraries, reference, and obtaining knowledge. For living, they prefer the country and not the city, as the preference is towards solitude, not crowds. A SEVEN may enjoy a book, over being with people. While they may be alone, they are not lonely, although they may fear loneliness. This individual is a good conversationalist when discussing a topic in which they are interested. A SEVEN appears mature (often beyond their years) and intellectual. They are quite intuitive and possess an inner guidance which springs from a deep source. Somewhat mystical, this person may obtain much information from dreams. While being intuitive, they also have a great interest in and obtain much information from the scientific. The SEVEN questions all and as a child, its favorite question may be "WHY?". This person maintains a quiet dignity and may be somewhat enigmatic. They are usually conservative in appearance and well-groomed. On the negative side, they may appear to be cold and aloof, unless comfortable with the people, place, or topic of conversation. There may also be a tendency towards being anti-social, crude, fearful, suspicious, and unreasonable. The negative SEVEN can be careless and unapproachable, almost hermetic in nature. They may have an undue interest in the bizarre which may be reflected in appearance or behavior.

EIGHT is the person who is sure of self and who exudes a power which may be off-putting to those who do not know the person. An EIGHT portrays the air of the executive and the leader, and is constantly looking for problems to solve. They tend to attract problems that need, and people who are seeking, guidance and answers. EIGHTs are dignified and businesslike in their presentation. They are people of ideas and leadership, not necessarily labor, although if in a situation where doing labor was required, they would perform to the best of their ability. An EIGHT is not naturally a subordinate and may chafe in that role. The natural tendency is to gravitate to management or ownership. This individual exhibits good judgment and has great potential to be a money-maker. The outward appearance is one of the successful person as EIGHTs desire power, wealth, privilege, prestige and control. For these reasons, they dress well and "dress to impress". They exude a strong, physical, and radiant appearance. Others will sense the power of the EIGHT when in their presence. The EIGHT who does not engage in the business world may be a good athlete with exceptional talent. On the negative side an EIGHT may be overly dynamic and flamboyant. There will be an element of anger, vindictiveness, and one of a person who abuses power. This person could be destructive and cruel or loud and obnoxious, as they attempt to impress others.

NINE is an ethereal, idealistic individual who is loved by all. The NINE is viewed as a humanitarian and a philanthropist, willing to solve the problems of the world. This is another vibration that will attract those looking for answers to their questions and problems. The NINE is "of the world" and is seen as one who belongs to all. Their approach may be idealistic, and at times, the harsh realities of the material world may be offensive to them. This individual portrays, and looks for, happiness and harmony in their surroundings and the people around them. The NINE is compassionate, emotional, and romantic. This person deeply cares for, and is very much "about" others. Being resilient and talented, they make good actors partly because the NINE encompasses all the characteristics of the other eight numbers on some level. This person holds a great appreciation of beauty and looks to create things of beauty and harmony. In its most positive sense, the NINE is unfailingly selfless. These are charming, warm, and outgoing people who are loved by others. There is a magnetic and personable quality that is an integral part of this person. A NINE maintains a youthful appearance that is both comfortable and casual. In its most negative state, the NINE is selfish and self-serving, egotistical and insensitive. They will tend towards carelessness and be possessive, moody and fearful. As opposed to being "of the people" they may very much be an attention seeker. They will exhibit narrow minded and foolish tendencies and may only seek out things for personal gain. In its worst case, this NINE may be violent.

ELEVEN is the "light messenger", the teacher of a higher vibration who is looked upon for answers and guidance from another plane. This is the first Master Number. They are seen as dreamy and somewhat detached, and may come across as if they do not feel as though they properly fit into the world in which they find themselves. Seen as inspirational and intuitive, the ELEVEN attracts others to its teachings. This person has strong faith in the self and their beliefs. If overly idealistic, their strong beliefs may tend towards "preaching" as opposed to teaching. This is a person who is both religious, creative, talented and artistic and who may be unusual and brilliant in their own way. The ELEVEN is more spiritual than materialistic and may be quite individualistic and unique. The negative side of this number is inconsiderate, egotistical and narcissistic. They may be prone to pouting. They must protect against being a doormat as Master Numbers not manifested on the higher plane will reduce to the worst conditions of the single digit number (in this case the 2). The ELEVEN must guard against high expectations as this may lead to disappointments and frustration. A negative ELEVEN may lack patience and be somewhat self-destructive.

TWENTY-TWO is the solver of problems and the builder of new and better worlds. In the same way that the ELEVEN may attract followers and students, the TWENTY-TWO will also be looked to for answers. Their work is geared toward improving the condition and appearance of the entire world and they must remain focused on the task at hand. If too self-serving, they will create problems and obstructions in all aspects of their life. The TWENTY-TWO must remain aware of their abilities and use them for the good of all. In this regard, it may find that it must be the most selfless of all the Master Numbers.

THIRTY-THREE vibrates on the level of the spiritual leader or avatar. This individual attracts both followers and opponents to their healing energy and teachings. This is a person of spiritual giving and kindness. They are, and must be sensitive to others' needs, desires and feelings. A THIRTY-THREE must hold consideration for all life and all things of the world. For this reason, they may be absorbed in nature. A THIRTY-THREE gives freely of themselves and are not looking for reward. They are gentle and kind. They must be aware of being a martyr to themselves and of becoming too much the egotist in their appearance and presentation.

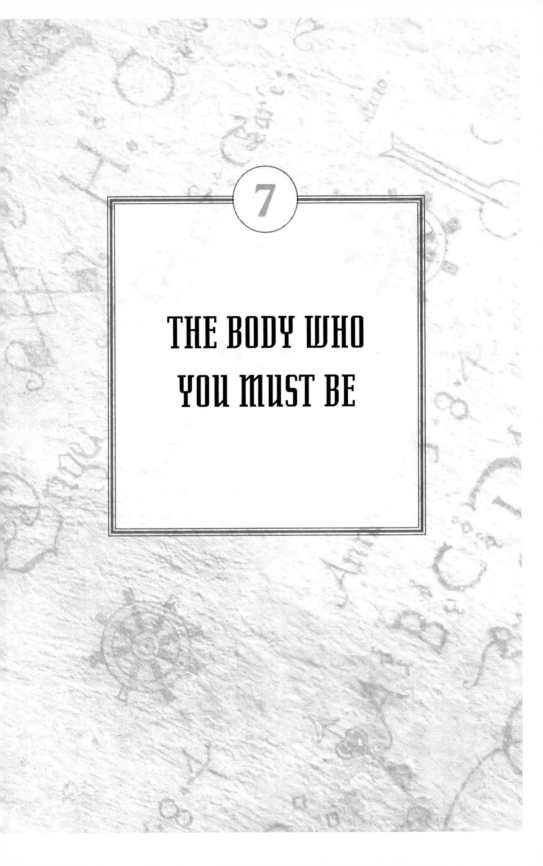

7

THE BODY WHO
YOU MUST BE

CHAPTER SEVEN

THE EXPRESSION-
THE BODY WHO YOU MUST BE

EXPRESSION/DESTINY- This is your BODY, the result of being and doing, which ultimately produces the perfect conditions. This is the integration of the soul and the personality into a combined spiritual and physical form. It is the BEING (Soul Urge) of your energy manifested in this plane through the DOING (Personality/Image). It is the ultimate expression of your total energy as a manifest entity here on Earth. By skillfully and lovingly combining your heart's desires into their ultimate physical manifestation, are you then able to fully exercise the SELF that you are, as a part of, and in relationship to, GOD. The function of the body is to act out that choice which you have made. This is the entire entity, the mind, and the body, the spirit- the holy trinity. THIS IS WHO YOU MUST BE, AND HOW YOU WILL DO IT! The expression is the essence of EXPERIENCE. The expression is the embodiment of the greatest talents, abilities, capabilities and possibilities of who you are. The number represents the type of work with which you will be most comfortable. It is the ambitions and achievements possible in this lifetime. The expression is your mission on Earth and represents what must be done for others.

	2		17/8		8		18/⑨
1	1	3	5 9	6	1	1	
BARACK		**HUSSEIN**		**OBAMA**			19//⟨1⟩
2 9 3 2	8	11	5	2	4		
16/7		15/6		6			19/ 1
9		14/5		14/5			

In computing the Expression, you must calculate the Soul Urge and the Image/Personality number for each individual name (first, middle, and last) reducing each to a single digit (unless it becomes a Master Number). You then add the Soul Urge and Image/Personality together for each name. In this example, add 2 + 7 of the first name to obtain **9**. Add the **8 + 6** of the middle name to obtain **(14)5**. Then add the **8 + 6** of the last name to obtain **(14)5**. Then add the **9 + 5 + 5 = 20**. Add the **2 + 0** to obtain **2**.

ONE – The ONE expression is the born leader. This is the pioneer, one who is unique and individual with an inventive mind. This person is the natural problem solver. A ONE is more concerned with self and may be quite single-minded in purpose. This number needs to be in the lead and is much more a beginner, not a finisher leaving the details to others. The ONE is very much "in the moment", demanding action and decisive behavior. This individual exhibits humor combined with a warm and altruistic outlook. He moves forward in a very courageous manner and may be quite good at making money. Expect strong opinions and feelings from a ONE, as they believe in themselves as natural leaders and originators. Negative characteristics of this number are a tendency towards being a bully. Other negative characteristics are that the individual may be bossy, impatient, grandiose, aggressive, egotistical, dominating, unpleasant, dictatorial, and ruthless. The negative ONE may have an explosive temper, often caused by frustration and obstacles in their path. They may lose any gains which are obtained through careless behavior, foolishness, or gambling. They must learn to use restraint with money.

Possible careers for the ONE expression are: EXPLORER, INVENTOR, DIRECTOR, EXECUTIVE, OWNER, POLITICIAN, PIONEER, WRITER, DESIGNER, ARTIST.

TWO – Whereas the ONE expression is the born leader, the TWO expression is the planner, the organizer, and the one who will work behind the scenes to ensure the success of whomever may be in charge. The TWO is tactful, patient, cooperative, and harmonious. Diplomatic by nature, they are not forceful in their personality or their actions. The position they assume will be centrist, not extremist. This person is emotional and often ruled by their emotion. They are thoughtful and courteous, and desirous of peace and harmony. The TWO appears even-tempered, poised, charming, and warm in demeanor and actions. This person makes a good partner as they tend to be supportive of those that they love, or those who may be in a position of power over them. A TWO is passive, cautious, and careful. They are most competent in that which they choose to do. With money, they may be thrifty and frugal. This individual is more apt to be guided by their heart over their head. The TWO is more a homebody than a traveler. Negative characteristics of the TWO are a tendency to be oversensitive and easily upset or hurt. They may become too dependent on others and exhibit co-dependent tendencies. At the worst they may be selfish, stubborn, and sneaky. They might also be a liar or resort to thievery and thuggery.

Possible career choices for the TWO expression are: POLITICIAN, DIPLOMAT, JUDGE, MODERATOR, TEACHER, ACCOUNTANT, PSYCHOLOGIST, JEWELER, MECHANIC, SCULPTOR, DANCER, CIVIL SERVANT, HOME AIDE, WORK REQUIRING DETAIL.

THREE – is the individual who is inspirational, creative, and sought out by others to uplift the energy of a situation or project. This person is filled with vitality and charm and will tend to be attractive. The THREE expresses a definite joie de vivre, an unbounded joy and appreciation for life. They are self-expressive, creative, and artistic with a magnetic personality. This person is also quick thinking and quick witted which is why many THREEs choose a career in the entertainment field. They desire to inspire and uplift through their creative pursuits and they are blessed with a generally optimistic attitude. This person thrives in an environment which is orderly and clean. The person with the THREE expression is a social person who loves easily and is easily loved. They are loyal and true if they are "in love". This person is an easy conversationalist, a quality that is enhanced by their changeable and flexible attitudes. The THREE expression is an ambitious person who does not like to be subordinate to others. On the negative side, the THREE can be quite a partier with a superficial and frivolous approach to life. They may be easily influenced by others and extravagant in a desire to impress, leading them to be a spendthrift. Other negative aspects may be that of a gossip, whiner, or complainer. There may be a tendency to be overly emotional and irresponsible with a lack of self-control.

A truly negative THREE will be deceitful, intolerant, and lacking in focus.

Possible careers for the THREE expression are: ENTERTAINER, WRITER, TEACHER, FASHION, DESIGN, SCRIPTWRITER, DECORATOR.

FOUR is the epitome of one who is stable and orderly. The FOUR expression is a builder of foundations, organizations, and structures. They are enduring, perseverant, honest, and durable. This is the manager, the person who sees to the implementation of details and designs. They are patient workers who work in a slow and steady manner until the task at hand is complete. Good with their hands, they tend to be mechanically inclined and usually excel in occupations that require the ability to use one's hands. The FOUR is calm and capable in stressful situations and accordingly they attract others due to their solidity. This person is a lifelong friend, if there is no deception or failure on someone's part to live up to image to which they are held. They are socially aware and may be somewhat dogmatic in their beliefs. The FOUR is careful and cautious and is generally not spontaneous in nature. This is the planner, the person who desires a course of action before moving forward. A negative FOUR will be a workaholic. They may be a worrier, as well as being jealous and petty. They will also be stubborn, intractable, antagonistic, and often vulgar.

Possible careers for the FOUR expression are: POLICE and LAW ENFORCEMENT, MILITARY, GOVERNMENT, CONSTRUCTION, MASONRY, TECHNICIAN, ARCHITECT, ENGINEER, FARMER, ECONOMIST, PLANNER.

FIVE is the person who lives for, and learns from, experience. This person is easily bored and quite curious. They will thrive in a situation where they have opportunities to be traveler. This is not an office worker as their restless nature will chafe with the restrictions of being in one spot, doing the same thing repeatedly. They work best in a job that requires movement. The FIVE needs constant stimulation and excitement. They are quite adaptable while being quick minded and quick acting. This person is impulsive, daring, action driven, and may get angry if restricted. This expression number is creative and their curiosity leads them to be a pioneer in new ventures. The FIVE is also drawn to social activity and they are a magnet to which others are drawn. They have great sexual appeal and will usually be attractive, even if in a somewhat off-beat manner. Their sexuality is often subtle but noticeable. In relationships, the FIVE must have independence and freedom. If provided this, they will be loyal companions and mates. Negative aspects of this expression are personalities that are moody, irritable, and high strung. They may be restless and shiftless, with a tendency towards pleasure above all else. They may also have a tendency to be outspoken, controversial and rude. Their curious nature and active minds may be hard for others to handle. The FIVE has a casual, live for the day attitude and consequently money comes and goes in their lives.

Potential careers for the FIVE expression are: DETECTIVE, SALESMAN, ENTREPRENEUR, ACTOR, LAWYER, LAW ENFORCEMENT, JUDGE, POLITICIAN, MUSICIAN, ADVERTISING & MARKETING, RACE CAR DRIVER (anything to do with speed), ARCHAELOGIST.

SIX is the number that thrives in positions of service to others. This number is the homemaker and is truly "the marrying kind". This person is friendly, and a loyal and trusted friend, thus making friends easily. A SIX has a great sense of responsibility and will gravitate toward and take on positions that require it. There is an idealistic quality that is a very strong part of this individual's make-up. They are very community oriented and become involved in local projects surrounding home, school and the town in which they reside. This also leads them to be a pillar of the community where they live. The SIX has a great appreciation for things of beauty, the home, marriage, family, the arts, music and literature, and all these things are enjoyed and loved. The person with this number is respectful of self and others. They embrace taking on responsibility for themselves, their family, and others, in some instances, even strangers. In so doing, they are loving and soft-spoken, as well as helpful and concerned, with the well-being of self and others. A caution with this number is that it may put self before others, often to detriment of themselves. The SIX is prudent and respectful and is not a risk taker. They are conscientious and may be demanding of self and others to behave in a way that is beneficial to all. Negative conditions of this number are tendencies to be smug, conceited, outspoken, and meddlesome. They may also be a worrier or exhibit co-dependent behavior in relationships. Also in relationships, they should be aware of being jealous or a domestic tyrant. Other strong negative traits are that the person may be overly opinionated and stubborn and likely to dig in their heels, creating situations where they then have difficulty retracting their position.

Potential careers for the SIX expression are: TEACHER, NURSE, DOCTOR, COUNSELOR, LANDSCAPER, DENTIST. PARENT, REAL ESTATE, VETERANARIAN, PUBLIC SPEAKER, DAYCARE, MEDIA.

SEVEN is the expression number of the psychic, medium, occult teacher or the spiritual counselor. This person is both philosophical and intellectual. Independent and desirous of privacy, this is solitary researcher, the seeker of knowledge, information, and wisdom. The SEVEN has a great interest in science, mathematics, analysis, and technology. He is the person who looks for the "why" of things and spends his life on a quest for understanding. Perfectionist by nature, the SEVEN may demand more of others than is possible as they have high standards and expectations of others. This is a number of trial and tribulation (as a reason for living). This individual is insightful and intuitive, possessing great understanding, sympathy and sensitivity to the people and the world in which he lives. The overwhelming desire to know and learn may lead to travel and adventure, as the SEVEN has an almost unquenchable thirst to unlock the secrets of the universe. With its keen and inquisitive mind, this individual is also a puzzle master. The SEVEN expression is not overly demonstrative although they possess a deep well of emotions. This person must find a way to express these emotions as it may lead to anger and frustration if not shown. They may usually be quiet and withdrawn, and are often labeled stuck-up or aloof. Because the SEVEN understands, they may appear unreasonable, as they expect others to do likewise. In consideration of their naturally introverted nature, they may seek compatibility more than love. They are not overly concerned with image, but more about what makes the person. With a keen mind, they are inquisitive and demanding of others, but they do not react kindly to same. In dealing with a SEVEN, one must understand that they will reveal themselves in their own time and on their own terms. If pushed or confronted with nosy people, they may be inclined to withdraw deeper into their shell. Negative characteristics of the SEVEN are a tendency to be sarcastic, unreasonable and argumentative. They may also be shifty, a schemer, a liar, or abusive. Because of their ability to discern the person below the surface, they may use that information in a manipulative fashion.

Potential careers for the SEVEN expression are: WRITER, EDITOR, TEACHER, LAWYER, SCIENTIST, RESEARCHER, COUNSELOR, ADMINSTRATOR, JUDGE, SPIRITUAL TEACHER or LEADER,

LIBRARIAN, ANTIQUARIAN, ANTIQUE DEALER, ART COLLECTOR.

EIGHT is the single digit master number that operates on a higher material plane and also represents the material and the spiritual. This number is definitely a leader, not a follower. Consequently they gravitate towards the position of management, ownership, executive administrator, corporate executive, and entrepreneur. The EIGHT desires power, wealth, prestige, and standing in community. They are capable and efficient, confident and authoritarian. This person has a talent for making or losing money and their efforts will be met with either great success or great failure. The rewards should be equal to the effort which is put forth. This individual is noble in bearing and will have a commanding presence. Others will recognize who is in charge when an EIGHT is in the room. They have an intensity that will either attract or repel. The female who has the EIGHT expression may have initial difficulty with both men and women, as women will sense that they are not quite "one of the girls" and men may be intimidated by the power which they portray. Generally, this expression is generous and philanthropic. They also live for the challenge and will readily respond to a dare. This is a powerful energy and must be met with strength, or the tendency will be for the EIGHT to overwhelm those around them. They possess great stamina and energy and will continue working when others have stopped. Negative characteristics of this number are that of the worrier. This person may be irrational, ruthless, cruel, unscrupulous, and vindictive. Other negative traits are a tendency to be oppressive and possession of a violent temper and unchecked anger. It is never a good idea to cross an EIGHT. The truly negative EIGHT may be a religious zealot or a master criminal. Even though they are good with money, the dichotomy of the number is that it may also create financial problems. It must learn to balance the material and the spiritual in order to be successful.

Potential careers for the EIGHT expression are: BANKER, INVESTOR, FINANCIAL ADVISOR, EXECUTIVE, PROMOTER, ENTREPRENEUR, REAL ESTATE DEVELOPER, MUSICIAN, ATHLETE, MANAGEMENT/SUPERVISOR, JUDGE, POLITICIAN,

NINE – this is the number that is the caretaker of humanity. The NINE seeks to make all right in the world through the efforts of being a humanitarian, philanthropist, and inspirational leader. This person is idealistic, sensitive and compassionate and consequently is prone to suffer with the world. They are mystical and intuitive and more about others than themselves. The NINE can combine all the best and worst of all previous numbers. Because it is the sum of the numbers 1-8 added together, it is all there can be and is. It has the ability to be or do anything in which there is great interest or talent. This is the number that perceives all the goodness and all the darkness that exists. It will live its life with high ideals and goals, always looking for the way to help and improve those around them, as well as the world in which they reside. Due to the inclusion of the attributes of all the numbers, the NINE must learn to effect a balance in its life. Negative traits which could manifest are a tendency to be impatient, egotistical, possessive, moody, restless, and insensitive. The negative NINE can be destructive with an impulsive and explosive temper. This person is highly impressionable and prone to strong outside influences.

Potential careers for the NINE expression are: ARTIST, ENTERTAINER, NURSE, DOCTOR, LEGAL, LAW ENFORCEMENT, POLITICIAN, PREACHER, SOCIAL REFORMER, ADVOCATE, LECTURER, WRITER, TEACHER, ACTOR.

ELEVEN is the first double digit Master Number. The energy of this number is that of the intuitive counselor, teacher and inspirational leader. It is idealistic and compassionate and is best in positions or situations where the goal is the improvement of others and society. The ELEVEN receives information from a higher plane so may appear at times to "not be of this world". They are visionary and a dreamer with inventive minds. It is these qualities they lead them to be teachers of religion or the occult. The ELEVEN is refined and elegant in nature. This is an independent person and is usually better working for themselves. They get along with all, but must be supported in their endeavors by those surrounding them. This individual has a good and attuned ability to attract, as they understand the laws of the universe even though money is not a primary concern. It is extremely important that this person must operate on the higher vibration of the 11 or risk be reduced to the worst characteristics of the base 2. Selfishness will create difficulties.

Potential careers for the ELEVEN expression are: VISIONARY, OCCULT TEACHER, COMMUNITY, NATIONAL or WORLD LEADER, TEACHER, PSYCHIC. PHILOSOPHER, ADVENTURER, RELIGIOUS LEADER, COUNSELOR.

TWENTY-TWO – the second Master Number is the universal man and the master builder. This person is purpose and goal driven with an ability to succeed on all planes. The person with the TWENTY-TWO expression is the humanitarian capable of helping mankind. They work in a "big" way as their purpose is to assist in the building of a new and better place for everyone. This person can relate and get along with everyone, but looks for people who can assist in the task at hand. Negative characteristics are those of a criminal and deceptive nature in business and behavior.

Potential careers for the TWENTY–TWO expression are: CONSTRUCTION, MAGNATE, TYCOON, NATIONAL LEADER, STATESMAN, PLANNER, BENEFACTOR.

THIRTY-THREE is the Master Number that represents the cosmic and intuitive healer. The vibration of this number is that of the spiritual leader, guru or avatar who is concerned with healing the individual and the planet. The THIRTY-THREE heals through teaching and a variety of healing modalities. This is the cosmic mother who takes responsibility for many. Because of this energy it will attract and repel the masses. This individual must guard against being moody, unrealistic, and becoming a martyr. It must remember that this is a very high calling and the intent is to heal.

Potential careers for the THIRTY-THREE expression are: DOCTOR, SURGEON, HOLISTIC HEALER, RELIGIOUS LEADER, TEACHER, NATIONAL or WORLD LEADER.

CHAPTER NOTE: When interpreting the Expression number, you must take into consideration the numbers of the Soul Urge and the Image/Personality combined to see what components make up the whole. Since the Soul Urge is the being, the "heart of hearts", it should be paid special attention. This is the direction the Soul would have the individual follow, and is the part which will make someone be truly happy. "Follow your heart" is the dictate that should be followed. The Image/Personality is the way in which the Soul Urge will manifest, as it is the doing energy. This must be looked at to find the most comfortable and companionable way to have the Soul Urge put forth. The Expression, being the sum of the parts, must find the path that enables the component energies to be best expressed. It should be read, "The Soul Urge working through the Image/Personality creates the Expression". The Soul Urge is the "spirit", the Image/Personality is the "mind", and the Expression is the "body". This produces the Body/Mind/Spirit trilogy.

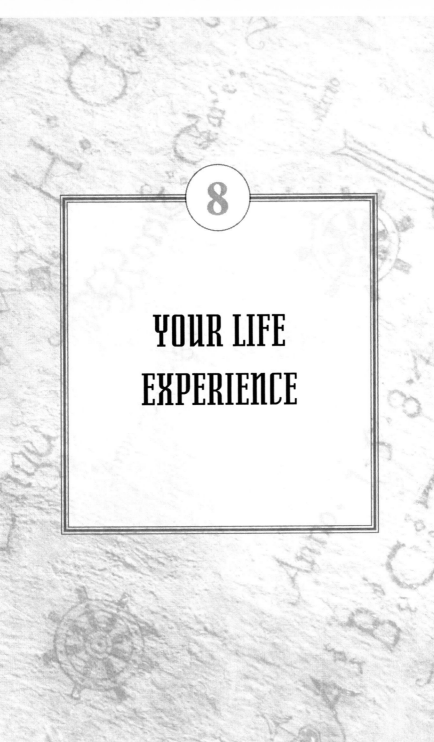

YOUR LIFE EXPERIENCE

8

CHAPTER EIGHT

THE BIRTH PATH/LIFE FORCE
YOUR LIFE EXPERIENCE

The Birth Path/Life Force number is your field of experience in this lifetime. It is the opportunities, environment and conditions you have chosen (through your date of birth) in which you have specifically chosen to exercise your manifest self. This is the road in life that you must travel. You can never change, or get off this road, since you cannot change your birth date. It is the culmination and accumulation of the Universal force/energy field which your Soul has chosen to use as a propellant on its' journey back to GOD. This is the sum of the experience of living and being in this lifetime, it is what happens to you. It represents all the opportunities and events in your existence. This is also a representative of your biggest fear...this is what you must learn!

To continue with our sample chart, Barack Obama's birth date is August 4, 1961. In setting up this part of the chart you would write the date this way:

$$8 \quad 4 \quad 17/8$$
$$8/4/1961 = \boxed{20/2} \rangle \quad \text{Life Path}$$

It is important to remember to reduce each number to a single digit (the exceptions would be if the number is an 11 or a 22, the Master Numbers which are never reduced). With the year, you must ALWAYS add the 4 digits to obtain a single digit, e.g. 1961 (add $1 + 9 + 6 + 1 = 17/8$) unless it reduces to an 11 or a 22. You then place the single digit over the appropriate section of the date: the month, the day, and the year. You then add the three numbers together, again reducing to a single number (unless it reduces to a 11, 22, 33, 44, or 55).

ONE – this is a lifetime of originality and individualism. Power, leadership, entrepreneur, executive ability, administrator, production. Motivation, creativity, inspiration. Determination, confidence, will power, ambition. Create and begin so others may finish. Outstanding talent and ability.

Negative: May lust for material success. Co-dependent if not strong. Lacks initiative. Boastful, lazy, stubborn, selfish, egotistical. Dislikes being told what to do. Troublemaker. NEEDS TO LEARN TO BE A MOTIVATED LEADER.

TWO – this is a lifetime of working in partnership and within the realm of dualism. Love, diplomatic, sensitivity. Friendly, helpful, cooperative, charming, considerate, works well with others. Carries out the tasks of others, often behind the scenes. Good partner. Neat, orderly, clean. Harmonious. Social. Dancer. Beauty, fame.

Negative: Pessimism, lethargy, depression. Sensitive, easily offended, overemotional, bad temper, shy, careless, sneaky, liar, coward, thief, cruel. NEEDS TO SERVE AND LEARN PARTNERSHIP.

THREE – this is a lifetime of creative expression and healing. Talented, cheerful, outgoing, enthusiastic. Good humor and wit. People pleaser. Entertainer, musician, writer, actor, dancer, public speaker, politician.

Negative: gossiper, talker, vain, jealous, critical, scattered, easily bored, worrier, no responsibility, work must be fun, not serious, extremist. Don't give up dreams and talent. Straying may lead to problems (self-esteem). NEEDS TO EXPRESS SELF CREATIVELY AND EMOTIONALLY.

FOUR – this is a lifetime of order, discipline and structure. Pillar of the community. Good partner for business or marriage. Practical. Organized, accurate, good/hard worker. Conscientious, conservative. Responsible, helpful. Family, country, duty, honor. Self-disciplined, it looks for this trait in others. Tailored and neat.

Negative: headstrong, opinionated, argumentative, too serious, intolerant, prejudiced, narrow-minded, workaholic, jealous, demanding, crude, ill tempered, needs proof (seeing is believing). Inhibited. May not be able to relax. Too demanding = martyr or tyrant. NEEDS TO CREATE ORDER AND STRUCTURE WITH RESPONSIBILITY.

FIVE – this is a lifetime of adventure, experience and change. Charming, popular, witty. Quick minded, adaptable, versatile, enthusiastic. Curious, analytical, interested, interesting, affectionate. Great salesman. Courageous, unafraid of the new and unknown. Pioneer. Innovator. Hands on. Learn from experience. Communicator.

Negative: overindulgence. Perverse. Rude and careless, irresponsible, restless, impatient. Takes unnecessary risks. Gambler. Beware of self-absorption and affect on others. NEEDS TO EMBRACE CHANGE AND LEARN TO KEEP IN BALANCE.

SIX – this is a lifetime of service and responsibility to others.

Nurturing. True friend. Advisor, counselor, healer, mother, sympathetic. Just, honorable, protective, concerned, nurturing, caring. Domestic, gardener, creative, artistic. Attractive, composed, poised. High ideals and standards. Career uses voice.

Negative: needs appreciation. Self-righteous, smug, interfering, always knows best. Stubborn, opinionated. Anxious, meddlesome, self-centered. Bossy, domineering, suspicious. Expects much. Child abuser. Sex offender. Beware of tendency toward co-dependent behavior and being an enabler. NEEDS TO LEARN, UNDERSTAND AND EMBRACE RESPONSIBILITY.

SEVEN – this is a lifetime of mental and spiritual exploration. Knowledge, advanced academic. Math, science, engineering, architecture, doctor, inventor. Succeeds through application of knowledge and talent (benefit to the world). Dignified, wise, silent. Quiet observer. Sees all, analyzes, understands. Solitude, books, libraries, nature. Strong beliefs based on knowledge. Must have proof. Good mind, inner strength, poised, refined, logical, intuitive, perfectionist. Teacher, professor. Interest in history, the past, old things. Refined elegance.

Negative: addictive, cold, aloof, inconsiderate, unapproachable. Sarcastic, slovenly, fearful, sneaky, tricky, gossip, cheat. Secretive, deceitful, brooder. Repressed emotionally. Stubborn. Loner. Mean, abusive, critical. NEEDS TO UNDERSTAND SELF AND USE KNOWLEDGE, WISDOM & INTUITION FOR SELF AND OTHERS.

EIGHT – this is a lifetime of business, executive and athletics. Wealth accumulation. Presents self well. Very capable, needs to be in charge. Big picture executive. Motivated, goal oriented, confident, ambitious, driven. Stamina, strength leads to athletics. Musical (performer or appreciator). Moneymaker, good with money. Potential to help many.

Negative: balance between material and personal. False impressions. Gigolo. Impatient, schemer, master criminal. Pushy, inconsiderate, thoughtless, overly materialistic. Anger and vindictive. Narcissistic. Spendthrift. Abusive. NEEDS TO UNDERSTAND MONEY AND THE ENERGY OF MONEY.

NINE – this is a lifetime of humanitarian service to others. Spirituality. Teacher, priest, artist, healer. Social worker. Magnetic personality, people person. Warm, loving, compassionate, empathetic, sympathetic. Universally loved and loving. Inspirational, idealistic. Logical, will-power. Imaginative, unlimited perspective and ideas. Selfless. Spiritual through action, not preaching.

Negative: impressionable, overly emotional, frustrated, selfish, unfulfilled, burdened, easily disappointed due to high ideals. Lacks understanding of others motives. Immoral, vulgar, liar, addictions. NEEDS TO LEARN HUMANITARIAN PURPOSE.

ELEVEN – this is a lifetime of inspirational and intuitive leadership and teaching. Enlightenment. Great dreams. Religious or spiritual leader. Interest in religion, spirituality, occult, the unknown. Deep connection to knowledge and wisdom. Inventive. Inspired, aware. Artistic. Often propelled by tragedy.

Negative: unattainable goals, frustration, fanatical, extreme, aimless, controlling. NEEDS TO LEARN THE DEPTH OF GIFTS AND HOW TO POSITIVELY USE THEM.

TWENTY-TWO – this is a lifetime of building a better world for all. Quite capable of grand accomplishment. Grand ideas built for the benefit of the many. A doer, not a dreamer. Powerful, peacemaker. Most important to put others before self. If not, result is troubles.

Negative: narrow-minded, inferiority complex, restless. Ulterior motives. Wicked, black magic, evil. Overly sensitive. Criminal mind and intent. NEEDS TO LEARN TO DIRECT ENERGY OUTWARD. REWARDS WILL FOLLOW SELFLESSNESS.

THIRTY-THREE – only occurred 182 times in the 20th century (out of over 36,500 dates). Those with a THIRTY-THREE Life Path, may find the early portion of their life (perhaps the entire first cycle) governed by the lower digit of 6. This will be a life of family and domesticity, although their career will in all probability be one of service to others. This person may find themselves feeling (and being perceived) as a little bit different than those around them. As the individual matures, the likelihood of the manifestation of the THIRTY-THREE energy will increase. It is at this time, that the person will find themselves turning more to a life geared toward healing, not only on the micro level, but also on the macro level.

Negative: This person must be sure to not enact martyr-like behavior. NEEDS TO LEARN THE POWER OF HEALING, SELF AND OTHERS. MUST NOT BE EGOTISTICAL IN WORKING WITH OTHERS.

FORTY-FOUR – this is the rarest of the Life Path numbers in recent history. It only occurred on November 22, in the years 1901 and 1910 (the only 11 Universal years during the 20th century. The next 11 Universal years began to occur during the 21st century with 2009, 2018, 2027, and 2036 and beyond). This will lead to a larger number of people with the FOURTY-FOUR life path in the 21st century, as more people will be entering this plane to assist with the transformations and paradigm shifts of the new century.

Negative: there is a strong caution to not become a meglomaniac and abusive in the use of power. NEEDS TO LEARN THE JUDICIOUS AND SELFLESS USE OF POWER.

FIFTY-FIVE – this Life Path is the second rarest Master Number Life Path in recent history. It only occurred on seven dates in the 20th century, and will not appear again for an extremely long time. The dates of this Life Path number would be November 22 in the years 1939, 1948, 1957, 1966, 1975, 1984, and 1993 (which were all 22 Universal years).

Negative: the caution is to exercise discretion and balance in all endeavors. NEEDS TO LEARN THE POWER OF CHANGE AND TRANSITION AND HOW TO APPLY THAT INFORMATION.

9

THE INCLUSION CHART

CHAPTER NINE

THE INCLUSION CHART

This chapter will explain the inclusion chart. How to set one up, and how to interpret it. It will explain how to use the chart to better understand the personality traits of someone and how to also understand the karmic/life lessons represented by the numbers that are missing. There are an average number of times that any given number will appear in a name. The most common numbers are 1's and 5's and the least common number is 7. If a chart has an overabundance of a particular numbers it will produce a trait that may be extreme. When a number is missing, it represents a lesson that must be learned.

In setting up the inclusion you draw a chart similar to a tic-tac-toe board.

1	2	3
4	5	6
7	8	9

In each individual square (top row, 1, 2, 3; second row 4, 5, 6; third row 7, 8, 9) you will place the number of times each number (1-9) appears in the spelling of the name. See our example on the following page.

$$\begin{array}{c} \text{1} \quad \text{1} \qquad \text{3} \quad \text{5} \text{9} \quad \text{6} \quad \text{1} \quad \text{1} \\ \hline \textbf{BARACK HUSSEIN OBAMA} \\ \hline \text{2} \quad \text{9} \quad \text{3} \text{2} \quad \text{8} \quad \text{11} \quad \text{5} \quad \text{2} \quad \text{4} \end{array}$$

6	3	2
1	1	1
X	1	2

a) CHARACTERISTICS OF PERSONALITY

The number of times any individual number appears in the spelling of a name will determine the strength of the characteristics defined in the following descriptions. A major number (the Soul Urge, the Image/Personality, or the Expression) will amplify the strength of the conditions described here.

1 – AVERAGE (3-4): Ones give someone a sense of self, and the ability to move forward in their life independently. They add the qualities of initiative, will power, individuality, and leadership. Ones provide the attributes necessary to be good in business. Ones also add wit and humor to a person.

MANY: If someone has more than an average number of Ones, they will have very strong opinions and fixed ideas. They may also have aggressive tendencies and a desire to have their own way. Too many Ones may create head and lung problems.

2 – AVERAGE (1): Twos provide the individual with compassion and patience as well as a willingness and ability to work with others. Twos provide the qualities of tact, diplomacy, and a cooperative nature.

MANY: More than an average number of Twos make someone very sensitive and shy. They will be a mediator with great patience. Many Twos may also create a talent for dancing, movement, and music, unless their shyness overwhelms them. They have a great appreciation of the arts. Work that is focused on history and culture may bring success. Many Twos may affect effeminate characteristics in a male. A great many Twos in a chart may make a person too adaptable and they may have an inner fear of people. The person with many Twos will find that having spiritual faith will bring about happiness. This is also a person who is detail-oriented and good in making arrangements. They will also be a romantic who possesses charm and grace.

3 – AVERAGE (1-2): Threes represent the capability of self-expression both written and spoken. This number also creates in a person enthusiasm, imagination, and creative talent. This person likes to do big things. An average number of Threes make a person happy and outgoing, although they must guard against too great a sense of elf-importance.

MANY: A person with many Threes will be someone who has outstanding talent, a positive imagination, as well as artistic abilities (music, painting, acting, writing, or designing). An especially large number of Threes will create impatience, too strong a self-interest, selfishness, and a lack of direction. Too much emotion will lead to too much talk or wasted endeavor. The person with a great many Threes does not like to perform hard physical labor, although they will work long and hard to obtain desired results if they are inspired.

4 – AVERAGE (1): Fours provide a level of organization, discipline, and work ethic in the individual. They also imbue the qualities of concentration, application, a good sense of practical values, and the ability to stay with things. This number also provides someone with a degree of order and systems.

MANY: The person with many Fours will be a good appraiser of value. They will have extremely good concentration. Their abilitiy to focus on details, structure, and work where effort required make them invaluable in work and projects. Too many Fours may bring about both pleasure and problems with their in-laws. The person with 3 or 4 Fours will be inclined to be a builder or involved in construction.

5 – AVERAGE (3-4): This is the most commonly occurring number in nu-merology. Fives provide the ability to change and transition in one's life. Fives enjoy travel and freedom as well as a need for fun and excitement. They also allow a person to be adaptable and flexible in situations.

MANY: Too many Fives will create restlessness and a lack of application. This person will have scattered interests and may find it difficult to concentrate on the task at hand. In many instances, they will have many projects going at the same time, often bouncing from one to another regularly. Too many Fives creates a bohemian nature and a wanderlust. This person will receive good opportunities through legal work or sales. This person is not likely to be domestically inclined unless there is variety or interesting people. They need a line of business which promotes travel and contact with many people. Too many Fives may make a person critical to a fault. They may be high strung and possess a very strong degree and interest in sex and sexuality.

6 – AVERAGE (1): Sixes provide an individual with a sense of family and responsibility. The person with an average number of Sixes will be a humanitarian, idealist, teacher, physician, nurse or be interested in children or welfare work. They love the home, as well as comfort and luxury. This person will have a keen sense of right and wrong. They will also possess a willingness to take on responsibility.

MANY: The person with too many Sixes will possess strong opinions and fixed ideals that are not easily relinquished. They will be stubborn and may be strict, dominant and demanding. A loss of ideals will break their spirit and may cause confusion. The person with many Sixes will possess a natural tendency for the persuasion of ideals and concepts. This person will also be imbued with a sense of generosity and humanitarian spirit. They expect loyalty from others. There will also exist a strong affinity for traditions. Radical ideals may mark the nature and position in life.

7 – AVERAGE (0-1): Sevens represent intellectual and spiritual analysis, techniques, investigations, and the power of observation. Sevens need to know WHY? This creates a questioning attitude. This person will possess a keen mind and will be one who desires to look beneath the surface. They will be skeptical by nature. Sevens add a degree of discrimination in actions as well as a sense of perfection.

MANY: The person with many Sevens has a natural tendency toward being a scientist, researcher, technician, or mathematician. This person will possess great intuition and perception. They will be skillful, selective and mentally clever. They will look to perform specialized work. Many Sevens may make a person difficult to know and create a situation where "what you see is not what you get". This person may also hold odd and unusual ideas and beliefs. If there is a lack of education, it may lead to schemes and hidden undertakings. This is a person who may want the best but who will also be close with money. Many Sevens make some-one a thinker who may often solve problems using their intuition. This is also an individual who dislikes showing emotions, even though they may possess very deep emotions. Too many Sevens will create doubt, fear, a distance in personal relationships, and inability to talk on a personal level.

8 – AVERAGE (0-1): Eights provide a person with a sense of personal power, self-sufficiency, as well as a businesslike ability to lead and supervise. Eights lend a sense of authority and strong will and they may appear dominant. This is a person who will also be independent in thought and action with a sense of balance and an ability to see both sides. They may be philosophical with a knowledge of "...*As above, so below; as within, so without*". This is not an easy number and strain about money may create problems. Eights provide a person a degree of control and an ability to rise to meet challenges. This person must also cultivate business training and a talent for money evaluation.

MANY: Many Eights will make a person intense, perhaps possessing too much drive and determination. The person with many Eights is an executive who is a good judge of character who will also coordinate the activities of others. This number will assist in making a person a good counselor and researcher with literary ability. Many Eights may also create a life that may be hard and frustrating and includes many personal tests. Mental energy should be expressed with inner poise and less discontent. Rewards are offered through the public and may include recognition and a standing in the community. A very large number of Eights will create a person who is overanxious and possesses a fear of failure as well as an inferiority complex. More than an average number of Eights will also display a tendency towards great worry about life, and especially money.

9 – AVERAGE (3-4): Nines give an individual the qualities of humanitarianism and philanthropy. This is the number which represents the brotherhood of man. Nine is an energy that is necessary to prevent total destruction. Nines afford a person with a sense of compassion, tolerance, benevolence, and goodwill. This number provides the color and drama of life. Nines provide a person with an ability to understand. They also make a person impressionable, intuitive, and possessing deep feeling.

MANY: Many Nines provide an extremely high degree of impressionability, imagination and generosity. The person with a large number of Nines may lack direction and a balance of feeling, thought and action. There may be a tendency to follow dreams without practical direction or emotional balance. Many Nines add beauty, warmth, and inspiration. This will also be a person with whom it may not be easy to reason. If a person has 6 or more Nines, they will be moody, overly sensitive, and not well physically. They will have flashes of intuition but may be lacking in common sense. It is important that the person who has this many Nines avoids food and drink during disappointments.

b) THE LESSONS

Lessons are indicated by the lack of a particular number in a chart. These are places in life and in the personality to which the individual must pay attention, and appropriately direct the energy towards improving the particular condition. Often called "karmic lessons", the absence of a number is an indication of something that was either done to excess, or not at all in a previous lifetime. When reading a chart, you must look to see if the number(s) missing in the spelling of the name, are present in the major numbers (the Soul Urge, the Image/Personality and the Expression). If the missing number(s) is one of the major numbers then the severity of the lesson may be mitigated somewhat. Since these are lessons, they may be learned at any time during the lifetime of the person. Some of the lessons (4 and 6) may be learned through the process of maturing and taking on the disciplines of work and family. It would obviously be easier if the individual can learn the particular lessons sooner, rather that later.

1. When the One is missing, it represents the inability of someone to to stand up for themselves and their rights. This creates a dynamic where the person is easy going, charming and lovely. They may be more interested in others than they are themselves. This individual may lack drive and ambition. If a chart has 0-2 Ones, the person will probably have a self-deprecating sense of humor. This will be increased if there are Twos present in the name.

THE LESSON *in the absence of Ones is that this person must learn to develop a better sense of self, gaining self-confidence in the process.*

2. When a chart is missing Twos, this shows that the person may be lacking in consideration for others. They will also exhibit impatience, tact, as well as a lack of tact and a sense of true cooperation.

THE LESSON *this person must learn is patience with, and tolerance of, others.*

3. Missing Threes in a chart will indicate a person with who is lacking in fanciful ideas, sentimental speech, romance, and imagination. These conditions will not be natural tendencies. Doubt, fear, and lack of self-expression will also be overwhelming tendencies. A tendency toward dullness and rigidity may also be exhibited. Lacking Threes will also invariably create problems in interpersonal relationships as the person will find it virtually impossible to express their thoughts and feelings. The result may be a tendency to yell and argue as a personal defense, to cover the inadequacy. A dichotomy may exist in that the person may very well have no problem expressing themselves in the context of their job or career.

THE LESSON *this person must learn is the art of self-expression, both personally and creatively.*

4. The person who is lacking Fours in the spelling of their name will demonstrate a lack of concentration and discipline. The lack of application may be a weakness of their nature. They will receive help through others but must learn to organize and construct their lives. No Fours create laziness and a dislike of order. There may be a tendency towards extravagance.

THE LESSON *is that this person must learn the traits of discipline, organization and how to work.*

5. If a chart is missing Fives, the person will exhibit timidity and a dislike of crowds and will have a desire to be alone. This person is afraid to face the world and will not be very adaptable. There may also be a lack of vulnerability. There will also be an overriding fear of change and an inability to adjust. They are quite content to have things remain the way they always were.

THE LESSON *is that this person must learn to embrace life and change.*

6. Missing Sixes indicate a weak sense of duty and responsibility. For this reason, domestic life may be taken lightly. This person must learn to accept that actions will only be reciprocated and not offered by others willingly. There is a caution to guard against codependent behavior. There may be many interesting situations and happenings when the Six is missing. No Sixes may also indicate a person of doubtful integrity and loyalty. Another condition may indicate a non-existent or strained relationship with a parent or parents, often the parent of the opposite sex.

THE LESSON *is that this person must learn to develop a sense of responsibility and family, while becoming dependent on themselves to establish their position in life.*

7. In Numerology, Seven is the most commonly missing number in the spelling of names. The person with missing Sevens will be open-minded and may experience more inner happiness. This person may be driven to better understand life, but not know which path to follow. It is the author's belief that the prevalence of missing Sevens in the spelling of names during the twentieth century is one of the driving forces behind the metaphysical/New Age movement and the desire of individuals to better understand themselves and the world in which they reside.

THE LESSON *for this person is that they must learn to become more in tune with self and the world through a spiritual or religious pursuit and belief.*

8. Eights are the second most commonly missing number in Numerology. The person who is missing this number lacks self-control and may be dependent on others. A positive aspect of this number missing is less strain after money in the long run. This eases the pressure of living and finances. This person may have a dislike of finance and handling money. They may have an "easy come, easy go" attitude towards money and life. Missing Eights may attract help and experience luck through others.

This person may also be lacking in a sense of personal power and inner strength.

THE LESSON *is that this person must develop a better sense of personal power and become comfortable handling money.*

9. The person who is missing Nines lacks broadness, tolerance, and compassion. This person may also have a tendency to be selfish. They may be helpful, kind, and capable without experiencing any feeling of universal forgiveness. Missing Nines limits the extent of accomplishment that may be felt. In order to expand their view of humanity, studies of comparative behaviors, religions, and character analysis will be helpful.

THE LESSON is *that this person must learn to be more magnanimous and humanitarian in belief and action. They must broaden their perspective of the world in which they reside.*

10

THE
CHALLENGES

CHAPTER TEN

THE CHALLENGES

THE CHALLENGES-*OBSTACLES TO WHOLENESS.* They are the real issues of life, the types of behavioral patterns and situations that might place a person into therapy. I attach a great deal of importance to the Challenge numbers. The challenge is derived from the Birth Path components, and represents the only time in Numerology where subtraction is the mathematical process used. The Challenges represent major stumbling blocks on the road of life that is the Birth Path. There are three minor, or sub-challenges, and one major challenge. The major challenge is a life lesson that remains until it is learned. The sub-challenges cover specific periods of time during the course of your life. If they are learned, they clear themselves and you continue in life unencumbered by them. If they are not handled and cleared, they will remain in your life, adding to the other challenges that come about, and the individual must deal with multiple issues in his or her life. Additionally, at all times the characteristics of the various challenges will be a part of the person's life adding the dynamics of the challenge to their life, thus affording the opportunity to work through and overcome/become the challenge(s) at any given time. Anytime a number appears more than once in the challenges, it amplifies itself and shows itself to be the one major issue which will prevent you from obtaining all your goals and all you desire in life. Everyone has a challenge to meet in life. Some have two, three, or four challenges, but one fact remains... they must be identified, met, and overcome if you are to gain the successes in life that you desire.

Challenges go from 0-8, and gain intensity and drama incrementally, as the number increases. The most common challenges are 1, 2, and 3. 4, 5, 6, 7, and 8 are less common but many times may show up as a sub-challenge, with a 1, 2, or 3 as the life challenge.

This is an important piece of information for any individual to gain from a numerology reading. It can help explain and identify the root cause for events in your life and better prepare you to understand, accept, and overcome/become them. Challenges may show up as personal feelings or bad habits, or they may be antagonistic behavior patterns that manifest as a lack of friends or associates, and in many cases, the challenges may manifest as "untrained behaviors" which have little or no use. The Challenges will also represent situations and conditions that exist in the family and interpersonal environment.

The Challenges can be compared to a "weak link in a chain" in that one weak link affects the strength of the entire chain, and a Challenge, once it is discovered, worked with, and strengthened can provide an impetus for constructive expression and success in your external affairs, as well as an improved internal situation with the "traumas" of life. If the Challenges are not dealt with they can sabotage your life and your successes. They represent underlying weaknesses that, with proper execution, when reversed become strengths.

The important thing to remember is that the challenge occurs below the Life Path, thus it affects the things of the material and three-dimensional plane. The lesson of the challenge is this: *RECOGNIZE IT...OVERCOME IT*....and then, *BECOME WHAT IT REPRESENTS.* At that time it becomes an *ASSET FOR FINANCIAL AND EMOTIONAL SUCCESS.* Challenges unmet, present the dynamic that creates the "I can't believe this is happening to me, again" scenario. These are internal issues, which will manifest in the everyday life of the individual. What needs to be done is for the individual to look inward at their fears and feelings and gain understanding of what is represented by the Challenges. If you are courageous enough to look at your life, then you must be courageous enough to take FULL responsibility for your life.

The solution in the realm of the Challenges is this: DIG and UNCOVER, DISCOVER, DON'T OVERCOME IT...BECOME IT!! ACCEPT IT. WORK WITH IT. BRING IT INTO HARMONY WITH YOUR TALENTS andHANDLE IT. YOUR ULTIMATE ANSWER TO HANDLING YOUR CHALLENGE(S) IS THE NUMBER OF THE DAY OF YOUR BIRTH.

CALCULATING THE CHALLENGES

As previously stated, in determining the Challenges, subtraction is the mathematical process involved. To calculate the Challenges you first subtract the number of the month of the birth from the number of the day of the birth. This provides you the first sub-challenge. The second sub-challenge is obtained by subtracting the day of the birth from the year of the birth. The third sub-challenge is obtained by subtracting the number of the first sub-challenge from the number of the second sub-challenge. The fourth and final challenge, or the Lifetime Challenge, is obtained by subtracting the month of the birth from the year of the birth. You must first reduce the birth date to three single digit numbers and proceed from that point. This is one of the only times in Numerology where you will reduce a Master Number to a single digit.

8 4 17/8

EXAMPLE: 8/4/1961

First, reduce each component to a single digit. The month is 8, the day of birth is a 4, and the year, 1961, reduces to an 8 ($1 + 9 + 6 + 1 = 17 = 6$).

1st Challenge–Subtract **8 - 4 = 4** (the month from the day)

2nd Challenge–Subtract **8 – 4 = 4** (the day from the year)

3rd Challenge–Subtract **4 – 4 = 0** (the 1st Challenge from the 2nd Challenge)

Lifetime Challenge–Subtract **8 – 8 = 0** (the month from the year)

In these calculations, you must remember to subtract the smaller number from the larger number. It does not matter which is the greater number, the important fact is the difference between the two.

The time frame covering the challenges is figured by subtracting the number of the Birth Path from the number 36. This calculation provides the number of years that the first challenge will be in effect. To determine the second challenge, add the number 9 to the ending year of the first challenge. The third challenge is determined by adding the number 9 to the ending year of the second challenge. The Lifetime Challenge is in effect for the entire life.

EXAMPLE:

With the birth date of 8/4/1961, the Birth Path is a 2. For the first challenge subtract $36 - 2 = 34$. The first challenge is in effect for the first 34 years of the life.

The second challenge is determined by adding $34 + 9 = 43$. The second challenge is in effect from the age of 34 to 43.

The third challenge is determined by adding $43 + 9 = 52$. The third challenge is in effect from the age of 43 to 52.

The lifetime challenge is in effect for the entire life, and is the most important for that reason. Although the time period for the 1st, 2nd, and 3rd challenges may cover a specific time, their effect will weave its way in and out of the life. As they are cleared, they will no longer be an issue. If they are not handled in their specific time period, their effect(s) may exacerbate.

WHAT THE CHALLENGES MEAN

1- Challenge of Independence and Individuality

Learn to stand on your own two feet. This is the challenge of self-respect in that you will stand your ground as opposed to doing what others want you to do. It is imperative that you give thought to what is good for all concerned and proceed accordingly. Understand who you are, develop your particular skills and talents, and BE YOURSELF. Be strong and be confident. Don't depend on others, but learn to respect authority, as you will have a tendency to butt heads with it. This is the challenge of authority when the individual is young (especially as the first challenge). There are indications of being raised in a strict or somewhat oppressive household, many times as a single child. You must develop a steady will and greater determination when it comes to matters of your life, but you must cultivate dignity and self-respect. You must take steps to stay away from feelings of resentment or inferiority.

HEALTH CHALLENGE: Matters of the eyes and the head, eyeglasses, migraines, eyestrain. Problems with the lungs. Nerves and nervous conditions usually cause the problems.

2- Challenge of Cooperation and Sensitivity

Shyness and meekness need to be overcome, and it is important that the individual develops the qualities of courtesy, consideration and patience. One will have to deal with hurt feelings, jealousy, and fear of people and learn how to handle the situations that are usually caused by impatience with the self and others, thus stifling any positive interactions. Tact and diplomacy must be learned while also learning to be thoughtful, obedient, devoted, and generous. BE YOURSELF IN THE COMPANY OF OTHERS, AND ALLOW THEM TO DO LIKEWISE.

Beware of a tendency to become a "doormat" for others, brought on by an inability or unwillingness to speak up for oneself.

As a first challenge in a female chart, it may be an indication of a "tomboy" type energy when young, oftentimes with a predominant male sibling influence. The woman may continue to exhibit "tomboy" type qualities throughout her life, often incorporating it into her femininity.

HEALTH CHALLENGE: Maladies and symptoms concerning the nose, ears, sinuses, breathing, lungs, hearing loss, and nervous conditions, the brain, and the solar plexus.

3- *Challenge of Self-Expression and Optimism*

This is a challenge of self-esteem and self-worth issues. One must learn to overcome any barriers (real or imagined) to fully and honestly expressing oneself. This may be caused by repression from others or a fear of appearing too forward. It is important that the individual is fully aware of his or her self-worth and be comfortable with contributing through the expression of their feelings and beliefs on whatever is going on. Learn to value what you have to offer. Do not bury the talents, but find a way to express them externally.

The 3 lends itself to creative activities involving words, art, music, etc. As a youngster, this challenge may create situations where intelligent children do not appear to adequately contribute in a learning situation. Parents must learn to engage their children in daily conversation/dialogue that will enable the child to learn how to express verbally. Introducing the child to creative endeavors early on and encouraging them to express themselves creatively will also help to diminish this challenge.

HEALTH CHALLENGE: Mouth, teeth, gums (usually due to neglect), sore throats, laryngitis, tonsils, and the liver.

4- Challenge of Self-Discipline and Control

The challenge of the 4 begins the increasing intensity of the situations involved with the particular challenge. This is the challenge of creating order and structure in your life. It represents learning how to discipline yourself to handle the tasks at hand. Structure, organization, and building foundations for the life you lead. It is important that you pay attention to the details, and establish system and routine in your life. Thoroughly do whatever is necessary to accomplish your goals and keep busy at them. In its most negative expression, a 4 Challenge may indicate that the individual will spend time in jail. As a first challenge this may be an indication of an individual coming from a family of origin that was very disciplined, often with a parent or influence from the military, the government, or law enforcement. Whenever the 4 challenge is present, it should provoke caution with vehicles and driving. Many times it will be an indication of an automobile accident, which is the Universe's way of getting the person to "pay attention". An individual with a 4 challenge, especially as the Lifetime Challenge, is particularly prone to what are known as "control issues". These issues may be either outwardly directed or received from others. The lesson here is to learn to establish appropriate boundaries with regards to your own life, and where you will "draw the line". These control issues may also be overt or covert, in other words, the individual may not even be totally aware of the control be in action. Coupled with a 6, 7, or 8 challenge, may represent some difficult times in personal relationships through 'dysfunctional' behavior patterns.

HEALTH CHALLENGE: The back, arm (right), legs, and skeletal system, and circulation. This challenge may also be prone to severe arthritis, or diseases such as Parkinson's, where control, or loss of control is the main symptom of the disease.

5- *The Challenge of Learning the Value and Meaning of Freedom and BALANCE*

This challenge cautions against the abuse of freedom and urges the individual to learn to use freedom correctly. Adjustment and change are two key words, and many times the individual will have a fear of change in his or her life. Opportunities for change will be presented and if refused, will become more and more dramatic and frequently lead to a situation where there will be no choice in the matter.... changes WILL have to be made. The key here is to develop the element of curiosity and learn to explore outside the artificial parameters that have been set. Learn to adjust to change easily and discard what is not useful in life. In the first position, the 5 challenge may be an indication of sexual abuse, and this should be looked at in context with the other challenge numbers, as well as the numbers in the inclusion chart. The 5 challenge will also indicate restrictions on freedom, and when coupled with a 4 challenge may show a very domineering and restrictive life situation. The other major aspect of this challenge is regarding "pleasures of the senses". With the number 5 being an indicator of the human condition, i.e. the five senses, caution must be taken regarding overindulging in pleasures of the sense, e.g. overeating, drinking, drugging, or engaging in promiscuous or wanton sexual pleasures. BALANCE is a key word with the 5 challenge.

HEALTH CHALLENGE: Stomach, sex organs, gall bladder, colitis, ulcers, and nervousness, also ailments that are connected to the five senses (eyes, ears, nose, etc.).

6- The Challenge of Responsibility and Service

The 6 challenge is the domestic challenge and of learning to appreciate those around you. The individual may be burdened with the care taking and responsibility of others and this responsibility must be accepted in a positive fashion, while taking care to not lose oneself in the process. There are positive and valuable lessons to be learned in these situations that will bring a fullness and richness to an individual's life. Caution must be taken that one does not become a doormat while administering to the needs of others, remembering that each of us has personal needs that must also be met. This challenge may also indicate situations of "co-dependency". These relationships may be with family members or in close, interpersonal relationships. The co-dependency may be emanating from the individual or directed towards them. A steadfast will and independence must be developed, so one does not slip into relationships where dependence upon one's mate is the major element for the relationship (the 'I can't live without you' type of energy). The 6 challenge also creates an attitude of "always being right" to the exclusion of all other viewpoints. There is a stubbornness and myopic, single-minded trait in the personality that will certainly create additional problems in both personal and professional relationships. A 6 challenge in the first position may also be an indication of an abusive background in the family of origin. The abuse usually taking form either physically, emotionally, or verbally. It may also be an indication of a separation or divorce in the family of origin. It may also indicate a divorce during the first part of the individual's life (this condition may also apply if the 6 appears as the 2nd or 3rd challenge).

HEALTH CHALLENGE: Heart, spine and neck, cancer, blood disorders, skin and anxiety.

7-Challenge of Analysis and Inner Guidance

With the 7 challenge the individual must overcome the feeling of aloneness and being separate from others and the world around him or her. The counsel here is to dig deeply and bring knowledge and guidance to the surface. Learn to question and not take things for absolute face value, and then follow your own intuition, or inner guidance, in discerning answers and a course of action. Develop, trust, and use your intuition. The call here is to develop the spiritual side and understanding of life. Encourage your spiritual nature and be ready and willing to use it for great benefit in your life.

As the first challenge, the 7 may be an indication of an element of addictive behavior being present in the family of origin, i.e. alcoholism, drugs, gambling, etc. If this condition does exist, then the individual is strongly cautioned that these types of behavior may also be a problem in their own life. As a lifetime challenge, particular attention must be paid to the element of addictions, and spiritual knowing and understanding must be used as tools to rise above the behavioral tendency. If coupled with a 6 challenge, the possibility exists of co-dependent relationships with people who have addictive tendencies. The 7 may also indicate a possible chance of learning disorders or difficulty in the educational process. It may also be an indication of an individual who is misunderstood, perhaps being misread by others. This would be brought on by the person's inability or unwillingness to discuss oneself.

HEALTH CHALLENGE: Kidneys, liquid organs, glands, white blood cells, and the sympathetic nervous system. Beware of drinking liquor and taking drugs.

8-Challenge of Judgment, Efficiency, Organization, and Self-Control

This is a very difficult challenge, as it is imperative that the individual learn to manage his or her affairs efficiently while exercising good judgment in all matters. Staying busy and focused are called for here, using reasoning for guidance, and taking care to see all things in their proper perspective. Intelligence must be used in a constructive manner, as well as the ability to see all sides of a particular question. The proper and judicious use of money and power must also be considered. In the first position, the 8 challenge may be an indication of coming from a family of origin, where someone had a great deal of rage or a very bad temper. A bad temper, rage, or vengeful behavior is also cautioned against in the individual with the 8 challenge. Since anger is misplaced power, it is important that the individual develops a strong sense of their own, personal power and manifest it accordingly, not in an abusive or dictatorial fashion. Understanding one's own power is called for here as well as an understanding of the repercussions of mis-using that power. The 8 controls the law of return and the law of karma, and it would be wise to understand that what is put out will be returned accordingly.

HEALTH CHALLENGE: High blood pressure, blood disorders, diabetes, colon maladies, hardening of the arteries, hereditary illnesses, the eyes, neurological disorders relating to control of the body's functions.

0-The Challenge of Choice and All Challenges

A 0 challenge indicates that there is either NOTHING overwhelming that needs to be worked on or that EVERYTHING needs to be worked on. This may be construed as a lifetime of constant struggles and issues, or that the lifetime is open for the individual to work on and perfect any portion of themselves that they choose. Opportunities exist to grow in all ways, as you have reached a point where you can choose what it is that you would like to work on. Do not take this lightly, or you will be tested when you least expect it.

HEALTH CHALLENGE: All the health challenges of the numbers 1-8 are within the realm of possibility, especially directed by the challenges that arise during the lifetime.

In conclusion, the challenges represent the issues of life, and accordingly must be given great regard with a concerted effort towards becoming the challenge so the rewards and benefits may be reaped. People who ignore or disregard the challenges are susceptible to the same condition or situation constantly manifesting itself in his or her own life. This will certainly impede growth and progress in life. By looking at the challenges, in relation to each other, and to the lessons indicated in the inclusion chart, a great deal may be learned about an individual. This is the area where the greatest breakthroughs may be made in unleashing an individual's full potential in his or her life.

NOTE: All the ailments and conditions listed under the specific challenge number may also be experienced with the corresponding Expression number.

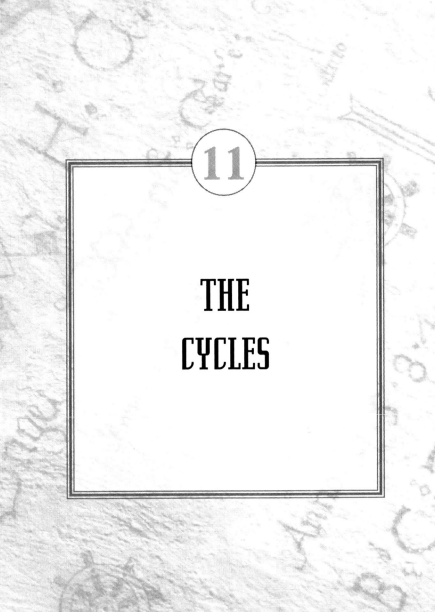

11

THE
CYCLES

CHAPTER ELEVEN

THE CYCLES

The three major Cycles are determined by the month, day, and year as represented in the birth date. They cover periods of time initially determined by the birth date. *The length of the first cycle is calculated by subtracting the Life Path number from 36.*

In the case of our sample chart for Barack Obama, 2 (the Life Path) would be subtracted from 36 making the time frame covered by the first cycle 34 years. The length of the second cycle (in all charts) is 27 years, meaning it would extend through the 61st year of his life. The third and final cycle would cover the remaining years of his life, no matter how long he lives.

1. OVERALL INFLUENCE: A ONE cycle is a cycle in which there is an increased and stronger influence on the efforts of the individual. This is a period of independence and individuality and a time to move forward fearlessly and be a leader. While it is alright to accept advice from others, it is important that you do not subjugate your ideas to the will or demands of others.

FIRST CYCLE: As a first cycle, independence must be balanced with dealing with authority. Since the influence here is for one to be strong-willed and dominant the individual may have difficulties with parents and teachers. This condition is especially magnified if ONE is the first, or the lifetime challenge. If there is a large FOUR influence (in the Inclusion Chart or the major numbers, especially the Image/Personality), physically aggressive behavior may develop. Difficulties may arise because of a clash between the desires of the individual versus the demands of authority.

MIDDLE CYCLE: When ONE is the influence of the middle cycle this creates a period that is both productive and satisfying. It is during this time that a person will "grow" into themselves. The person will also live an active life and the leaning would be towards being self-employed. Because of the ONE influence, partnerships may be difficult unless the partner is dedicated and committed to working towards a common goal.

LAST CYCLE: As a last cycle this will again be be an active and forward moving period. Under this influence the individual may find themselves working until the end of their life. There may be an element of frustration caused by the desire for action versus diminished physical capacities. It is during this period that mental capacities may increase. If not working for themselves, this will be a period of creation of new ideas for others. There is a possibility of living out the final years alone.

2. OVERALL INFLUENCE: A TWO cycle is a cycle in which the emphasis is placed upon working in partnership. It is during this cycle that it is important to come to terms with the duality of life. Details are important while learning patience, obedience, how to work with as well as taking a back seat to the efforts and plans of others.

FIRST CYCLE: During this cycle, there is a caution against being too oversensitive or emotional. There is a definite need for harmony in the environment to promote excellence in the actions, especially in school. A period will produce a child/student who is quite studious. There is a possibility that the home might be abusive and emotionally traumatic.

MIDDLE CYCLE: During this period, there may be an increased interest in politics, diplomacy, and doing the work of a counselor. This is definitely a time of service to others where the efforts are directed toward promoting the dreams and ideas of others. This is a good cycle for marriage and partnership.

FINAL CYCLE: As the final cycle, this is a quiet time devoted to hobbies and the collecting of things of interest. Antiques, and things from the past may be of increased interest. This is a favorable time for study and to be engaged in enjoyable pursuits and activities. This is a peaceful time filled with harmony with others and the surroundings. In all likelihood, the final cycle under the TWO will be spent living life with a partner.

3. **OVERALL INFLUENCE:** A THREE cycle is a period of increased creativity and self-expression. It is during this time frame that the individual will likely be involved in situations of a more social nature as well as pursuits of an artistic or entertaining nature. This condition may not be good for educational pursuits as there is too much concern with socialization and the child may be easily distracted.

FIRST CYCLE: Under the influence of the THREE cycle in the first position, the child may be overly expressive which may create suppression from adults and authorities in the classic example of a child should be "seen, and not heard". If combined with a three challenge, this may create difficulties with the self-expression and self-esteem. The child in a Three cycle will be intelligent and inquisitive and should be encouraged to pursue any artistic or creative talents. This is a cycle where the child may look to have a good time, which may interfere with learning and study. For this reason, involvement in the arts would be beneficial.

MIDDLE CYCLE: During this cycle, the person will be looking to enjoy life. The influence here is one of an easy money attractant which may lead the individual to be extravagant. Under this THREE influence the person looks for social activities and will excel in undertakings that are social in nature. This time frame is conducive for using words, written or spoken, and any artistic or creative talents. This is also a good marriage cycle.

FINAL CYCLE: As the final cycle, the THREE is a time of friendships, socialization, and enjoyment. It is during this period that the person may garner recognition and fame. As with all THREE cycles, this can be an artistic period. This is also a good time to travel and make contact with others, both old and new acquaintances. The overall energy of this period is one of progress and fun.

4. OVERALL INFLUENCE: A FOUR cycle is a period that may demand an increase in the work and organizational efforts of the individual. This is a time of creating the structure for the future. There can be great productivity during this cycle as the person works towards the goals and lays the foundations for the future. This is a time to develop routines and establish discipline. During the first two cycles under the FOUR, the person may gravitate towards a career in the military, law enforcement, or government work.

FIRST CYCLE: As a first cycle, the FOUR may be difficult for a child as it is counter-intuitive to the natural playfulness of a youngster. This may be a serious child who will be good doing chores and following a routine. This child will have good stamina and the ability to develop a good work ethic. If encouraged and taught, the child will also be able to develop a good degree of manual dexterity. In extreme instances, this may be a period of poverty and abuse. This child may be emotionally stunted and be a victim of too much discipline, especially if the first challenge is a FOUR. Overall, this child may be complex and unemotional.

MIDDLE CYCLE: This cycle is excellent for increasing the level of productivity but there may be tendency towards being a workaholic. The caution to be observed is that too much work may harm the health of the individual. This is a good cycle for saving money and establishing a strong financial foundation for the future. A slow and steady approach creates the desired results. This is also a good parent vibration but one must beware of establishing too much discipline in the raising of children. The FOUR cycle is a solid one for family, although the dominant energy may not be social or emotional creating situations that may be restrictive to the self and others.

LAST CYCLE: During the last cycle under the FOUR, work continues. Even after retirement, the individual may become involved in community affairs, politics, or various committees and organizations. During this cycle, the person may find that they must stay busy. With a final cycle of FOUR, taking care of others brings happiness.

5. OVERALL INFLUENCE: A FIVE cycle will be a cycle of increased activity, constant movement, and changes. This is a period of adaptability and variety and the individual may not settle in any one place or on any one thing. It should be known that one will keep moving and learn to adjust accordingly. A FIVE cycle is not necessarily good for relationships, as the desire for change may overwhelm any stability. During the period of any FIVE cycle, the individual must beware of abusing freedom and overindulging in "activities of the senses".

FIRST CYCLE: As a first cycle, the FIVE child may have difficulty because of innate curiosity and an overabundance of activity. This period demands and needs freedom and stimulation. The child with a FIVE as the first cycle will chafe at routine, reject responsibility and become easily bored. There is a possibility of this child being diagnosed as ADD, or ADHD (especially if the first Challenge is a FIVE, or if there is an abundance of Fives in the Inclusion chart, or a major FIVE, especially in the Image/Personality number). The individual will have a keen mind and will be inquisitive and learn quickly. It is important that the education of this child be diverse and interesting. Caution must be exercised in raising this child as it will try anything once. This child may be a late bloomer as it must learn to channel its curiosity and energy into a more focused direction. There exists a possibility of having divorced parents or even an emotionally ill parent. This is especially true if the first Challenge is a FIVE, SIX, or SEVEN.

MIDDLE CYCLE: During a middle cycle of FIVE the individual will be drawn to and will embrace travel, change, and numerous activities. Again there may be a tendency to reject responsibilities and this person may find it tough to settle down. This person will always be looking for new adventures and experiences and people with whom to share them.

Through focusing the energy, the individual will learn to adapt to changes and constructively release old patterns. During this period, the person will find that variety furthers the purpose of their life.

LAST CYCLE: Those with a last cycle of FIVE will not be found sitting at home watching life pass by as this an active period. This person will look to travel and meet new people while discovering new places. Routine and doing the "same old, same old" will create boredom so there will be a drive towards experiences and discoveries. There may be an increase in intellectual pursuits and well as an interest in eclectic hobbies or interests.

6. OVERALL INFLUENCE: A SIX cycle is a cycle in which the energy is more centered on service to others and responsibilities to family, friends, and community. It may feel somewhat restrictive because of the level of obligations that become a part of the life of the individual. There may be a tendency to feel burdened because of this, and the person must learn to accept these responsibilities and balance them with other aspects of life. The SIX cycle is a good time for marriage, family, love and devotion.

FIRST CYCLE: The child with a first cycle of SIX may feel burdened by an overwhelming sense of responsibility. While he will probably embrace this, he may feel as though he is missing out on "being a kid". This child will look for work as a baby-sitter, a waiter, or in any position in a service industry. There may also be a tendency in which this child will wish to stay at home, and they may not leave until later than a typical child. This individual will be quite helpful and be one with whom it is easy to get along. There may be a somewhat restrictive energy about this child and he may be a bit of a worrier. A condition of the SIX first cycle is that the child might be from a broken home or suffer from emotional, verbal or physical abuse, especially if the first Challenge is a SIX.

MIDDLE CYCLE: During this cycle, the individual will look to be putting down roots, getting married and creating a family with children. If career oriented, this person will enter the fields of nursing, teaching, counseling or any employment that includes service to, and doing for, others. This may be an artistic period, and if artistic or creative talents are present, the person should incorporate this activity into life. Any pursuit may call for hard work to accomplish that which is sought. Ideals may become a problem if the person attempts to impose them upon others.

LAST CYCLE: When the final cycle is a SIX the individual will be blessed with the rewards for lifetime of service and work. The life and environment will be loving, and the person will enjoy a good relationship with a mate, family, and friends. This should be a period of contentment and financial security, as well as recognition for the efforts that are put forth (in many instances, for work that was performed earlier in life). Once again, the person should accept the limitations and temper their responsibilities with boundaries.

7. OVERALL INFLUENCE: A SEVEN cycle will be a time for education, the pursuit of knowledge, research and understanding. It is important that a balance is created between the pursuit of the spiritual with the material. The rewards obtained are that which come to the person, and not pursued for the sake of pursuit. This period is blessed with an inner wisdom and understanding of the mysteries of life. There will be a desire for alone time and meditation. A caution: *If combined with a FIVE or SEVEN challenge, the person must beware of addictive behavior (drinking, drugs, gambling, sex, etc.).*

FIRST CYCLE: This is not an easy first cycle as the child may be misunderstood. There is an element of the young genius which may make it difficult for the child to feel as though he fits. This is not necessarily a social time, as it calls for being reserved and quiet. A trend towards "different" behavior may be a means for the child to join his friends and peers. This child may live in a world of his own as it follows the beat of a different drummer and will be thoughtful while waiting for inner guidance. In school, the child will most likely be studious and scholarly with an interest in science, math, research and the unknown/unseen. It is good for the parents to draw the child out and have him express his thoughts, otherwise he may become too introverted.

MIDDLE CYCLE: During this cycle, the study continues as an interest in books and education, research and analysis, and occult and spiritual becomes a foremost pursuit. This cycle is not great for relationships unless the partner is understanding and compassionate while being supportive of a person who may not be overly social in nature, as there will be a degree of being emotionally repressed. In this SEVEN cycle, the person must develop the talents to create income, as societal withdrawal will work against them in their endeavors.

LAST CYCLE: As a final cycle, the SEVEN is a quiet time spent studying and gaining knowledge. There will be an increased interest in philosophy, religion and spirituality. Since this is a period in which the person may be alone, they must caution against loneliness or becoming a hermit. During this cycle, the person will be sought out for knowledge and insight. There is a strong possibility that the individual may be widowed and live out their life alone.

8. OVERALL INFLUENCE: An EIGHT cycle will be a cycle in which the efforts create a period of business and moneymaking. The major concern will be with the material world, but it is important that the person must not forget the spiritual aspect of life. This will be a period of business opportunities and success will come through having control of the projects in which one is involved. During any EIGHT cycle, the individual must exercise a judicious use of power.

FIRST CYCLE: As a first cycle, the EIGHT may create difficulties for the individual and is the second most difficult number to have for a first cycle. Because of the power associated with this number, there may be an overwhelming sense of responsibility thrust upon the person. During this period, the person must learn judgment and the use of power. This child must learn to gain self-confidence and be educated in the understanding of behaviors and the consequences of those behaviors. This child may also need supervision until it learns the judicious use of its power. The child with the EIGHT as a first cycle should be a good student or athlete, but may need to overcome any self-doubt. This child may come from a home that has good financial standing. If coupled with an EIGHT challenge, this person should be aware of their temper. The individual must understand the concept that anger is misplaced power. In many instances, this person may use sex as a replacement for affection.

MIDDLE CYCLE: This cycle is a time in which the individual must learn to be practical and exercise an efficient use of time. This is an excellent period for projects that include big business and finance, and is a good time for the accumulation of wealth and assets. This period calls for making plans, following through, and reaping the rewards.

LAST CYCLE: The last cycle of EIGHT is a constructive period and a time of achievement. This person will stay active in business, management, or in activities that call for a use of the abilities. During a final cycle of EIGHT the individual needs to stay busy in some form. This person will remain energetic and may feel a lack of contentment if not doing something useful. This is a period calling for the management of affairs and, in some instances, the individual may pursue a new career.

9. OVERALL INFLUENCE: The NINE cycle is a period during which there will be a greater involvement in work and efforts of a more humanitarian nature. The NINE cycle calls for an element of selflessness when the individual puts others first. This may not be easy, because it calls for putting yourself second in your own life. As a person matures, they will understand that their rewards will appear through these selfless efforts. The NINE is a completion cycle and because of that it is hard for relationships because of the energy of an "ending vibration". These cycles may be times of great emotions.

FIRST CYCLE: This is the most difficult cycle to have as a first cycle. The child may feel alone and confused while experiencing intense and deeply emotional feelings. During this first cycle, many things of a karmic nature from previous life will be a major part of the existence. Relationships, jobs, etc will be short-lived and an intense nature. These experiences are of an intense nature as the individual "finishes up" the business that was carried forward. If this is the only NINE cycle in the chart, the person will have a somewhat easier life in the following years. There may be many disappointments through a lack of fulfillment of personal desires. This child will be helped if encouraged to pursue things of an artistic nature.

MIDDLE CYCLE: This cycle again holds the energy of being selfless. The individual must learn that the successes in their life will come through doing for others. The rewards of love will come from doing for others, and not through personal love affairs. During this cycle, the individual must not accept limitations, and should work for the good of all. This will be a period of idealism. Because of the influence of the NINE, there will be a lack of permanence in relationships and endeavors.

LAST CYCLE: The NINE cycle as the last cycle is a time of completion for all that has passed through the life of the individual. Much will pass and the person must learn to embrace the selfless nature for which this cycle calls. As with all NINE cycles, this is a time for artistic endeavors. By doing for others and contributing to others, will come the rewards, happiness, and satisfaction in life.

11. OVERALL INFLUENCE: The ELEVEN cycle will provide greater opportunities for public recognition, fame, and accomplishment along the lines of the true passions of the individual, especially as a middle or last cycle. In business during this cycle, the person would do well to have a business advisor/manager. The ELEVEN cycle is a time of revelation, inspiration, intuition, and inventiveness. These cycles will be a time of interest in the spiritual or occult. There may be opportunities for leadership or being a teacher.

FIRST CYCLE: For a child, this may be a difficult cycle because he has a foot in each world, that is the spiritual and the material that may create a situation in which the child may be lacking balance. This child may "hear and see" things that are real to the child, but not so obvious to those who surround him. Under the Eleven cycle, the child may be nervous and energetic and might withdraw because it feels different. This individual will be inspired and will learn quickly while discerning much in the world around them. There may be a degree of nervousness in the person's nature. For a child, the early influences of this cycle may be more in tune with the TWO cycle. The energy of the ELEVEN may begin to appear as the child matures.

MIDDLE CYCLE: It is during this cycle that the individual has the greatest influence in receiving fame, recognition, and great accomplishment. The work that is performed will attract the attention of many, and may lie more in the non-material than the material world. The rule to follow is to not seek fame, allow it to come to you. This is a time to teach and inspire. Partnerships may be good or bad, depending where the energy is focused. During this cycle the individual may experience a difficult time finding gainful employment, the focus will be on bettering the world. A caution is that heightened sensitivity may create health problems. It is important to maintain balance in all aspects of life.

LAST CYCLE: With the ELEVEN as the final cycle, the possibility of fame continues. The individual must work towards a greater understanding of others, but accept that the perceptions and beliefs may be different from those who surround him. There is a great energy that needs an outlet and one should cultivate the talents with people and through various pursuits. It is important to stay active, physically and mentally, and to be patient and tolerant with the situations and people in life. A generational energy (all people born during an ELEVEN Universal year share an ELEVEN last cycle) that possess the possibility of positively influencing the world. The energy of this cycle has more to do with spirituality than materialism.

22. OVERALL INFLUENCE: The TWENTY-TWO cycle is a period of time where great efforts will produce great results for the individual. This is a period of time that should be dedicated to the betterment of all. There is a tremendous power associated with this cycle and the person must remember that the only limitations are self. In restricting the self, one reduces to the energy of the TWENTY-TWO to the worst conditions of the FOUR. The guiding thought here is to think big and maintain a strong belief in the self and its' ideas. The person under the influence of the TWENTY-TWO cycle must be a leader who does not allow themselves to be controlled by others. This may be a difficult period and the individual must be prepared to handle the power and responsibility that are conditions of this cycle. There is good chance of success in all arenas, and it is important to use the rest of chart to determine the course of the life. Nervous energy must be channeled and the person should have faith in themselves and their plans and move forward. Relationships will be enjoyable and successful during this cycle if expectations of the partner are not measured against self. The person must direct their efforts and projects towards the "all" and success will be within reach. This is a cycle of high energy. A TWENTY-TWO cycle can never be the first cycle.

LAST CYCLE: During this cycle, the individual must find outlets for the power and energy that is available. It is important that one does not stay idle and continues to lead. This is a generational energy (1939, 1948, 1957, 1966, 1975, 1984, 1993), so great things can be accomplished by many for the all. This is a time of leadership that can have great impact on the entire world. Large plans need follow through by using the talents of the individual. It is important to maintain self-confidence and to not limit self, because the only limits are those which are self-imposed. This is a period that will be productive, successful, and rewarding.

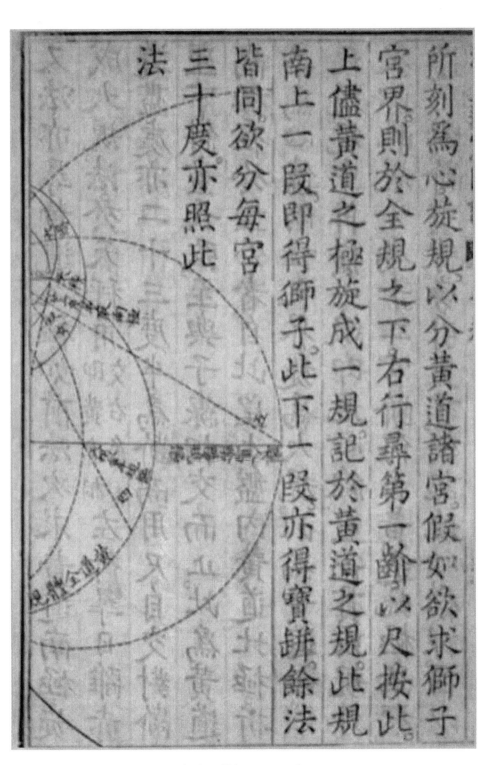

所刻為心旋規以分黃道諸宮候如欲求獅子
宮界則於全規之下右行尋第一齣以尺按此
上儘黃道之極旋成一規記於黃道之規此規
南上一段即得獅子此下一段亦得寶缾餘法
皆同欲分每宮
三十度亦照此
法

Ancient Chinese numerology

12

PERSONAL
YEARS

CHAPTER TWELVE

PERSONAL YEARS

Personal years are part of a continuum of nine-year cycles that make up the lifetime of an individual. These nine-year cycles are a constant opportunity to grow in your life, and the vibration of each succeeding year creates the energy to improve and correct as you proceed.

My favorite analogy for a nine-year cycle is to think of it as a garden. The first year is the time in which you decide to "plant a garden". You pick the spot to cultivate, decide what it is you wish to grow, purchase or obtain the appropriate tools to mplement your plan, and then you plant. If this garden is tended appropriately in each succeeding week, you will reap what you have sown at the end of the time period. And so it is with this cycle. In your first year, you should *plan and plant your garden*. If you follow the appropriate steps and adhere to your plan, you should reap what you have sown in your eighth and ninth years.

A personal year extends from birthday to birthday of each year and does not track the calendar year as we know it. Each year operates under the vibration of a number from 1 to 9 (there may be an occasional 11 or 22 personal year). To determine your personal year, take the number of your birth month, add to it the day of your birth, and add that to the number of the year, e.g. 2009 is an 11. This will give you your personal year number.

EXAMPLE: Your birth date is August 4. The current year is 2009. August is the 8th month, 4 is the day, and the year is 2009, which is an 11.

$$\text{Add } 8 + 4 + 11 = 23$$
$$2 + 3 = 5$$

5 is the personal year.

1. *Take action, plan and plant.* The ONE year is the first year of the cycle and is a year of beginnings. This is the year to plot a course for the next nine years and a time to set goals and determine a course of action to reach those goals. You are encouraged to have faith in yourself and do not doubt, stall or vacillate. This is a time to move forward as your progress will be made through your personal efforts. This year brings about new ideas, friends, and businesses. The encouragement here is to do something new as you will be presented with favorable opportunities. The ONE year is the time to plan and make changes. The encouragement is to work and avoid laziness. Things will not come about easily, as work will be required to implement plans and create the beginning of what you plan and desire.

2. *Be receptive, work with others.* The TWO year begins the growing process of your plans. This year calls for patience. It is a year to study,

learn, and work in partnership, sharing and cooperation with others. It will be important that you work to see both sides and the duality in situations. Work to cultivate friendships and new associations. This is a time for the good life, but the caution is to not be frivolous in your actions. During this year, if you help others you will receive help in return. There is in play the law of attraction, not action. It is important to pay attention to the details, get affairs in order, and pay debts. The individual must exhibit a willingness to wait. It is important to remember that tugging on a plant will not hasten its growth. Trying too hard will not bring desired results.

3. *Be creative in moving forward and concentrate on improvement.* The THREE year is a year in which one should put their best foot forward and cultivate friends and associations. There may be much in the way of entertainment and socializing, and one should work to remain cheerful and optimistic. This is a time to use creativity, inspiration and imagination to accomplish and further goals. Be aware that too much emotion will waste time. In the THREE year the person will obtain help through friends and family. This is a good year for making money, receiving opportunities, falling in love, traveling, enjoying pleasure, and gaining popularity. There is a caution to beware of being extravagant. The THREE year is a good time for public speaking, writing and publishing. By promoting these endeavors, the result will bring opportunities. Take care to not scatter the energy too widely and be careful to not indulge in too much partying. This is the year when ventures and projects begin to bloom. In relationships, there will be a deepening of love and life will present reasons for optimism.

4. *Work hard, take care of details and organize.* The FOUR year is a year to work. The energy of this year will mean that one should be more practical and partake in more work and less pleasure. During this time period is when a foundation for security should be implemented. This is a time to build homes, lives and property. Carelessness will bring about longterm problems. Use this year to shore up the structure and foundation of ideas and plans. Dig in and make corrections, while concentrating on the details of plans, projects, and ideas. Keep busy, work efficiently, and stay in a state of action, doing what needs to be done to further things along. This is also a time to put the affairs of life and business in order. Exercise self-discipline and beware of too much rigidity. There is a caution to pay attention to issues surrounding health.

5. *Be prepared for changes, make adjustments.* The FIVE year is the middle year of the nine-year cycle. This is a year to make adjustments and changes where necessary. Activity may increase in all aspects of life and it is important to not lose focus. During the FIVE year, there may be a possible move or a change of job. The year will bring new experiences, new challenges, and new people into the life. The energy is directed towards change, growth and travel. There will be opportunities presented outside of the routine of normal life. The urging here is to let go of the old, as the new is arriving. In all endeavors, this is a time to promote, market and advertise. Progress is at hand and changes should be advantageous. Be cognizant of restlessness and impatience towards anything that may hold you back. Be sure to channel the energy and don't scatter it into a multitude of projects. This is a renewing time and is a step towards a fuller life. Be resourceful and take advantage of the changes that may manifest. The caution is to be aware that this year may be a bit unsettling or uncertain. This may be the year where it is time for a vacation and it is a time to incorporate some fun into work and activities.

6. *Work towards harmony.* The SIX year is the year to resume and accept responsibility. This year is the time to reign in the expansion and energy from the FIVE year. There may be unforeseen obligations that require duty and the care of a family member, perhaps because of illness. This is a year of selfless service to home, community, charity and humanity, and you may be called upon to help others. There will be a increase in the desire for domesticity and interpersonal relationships. This is a good year to take on projects around the home and family. A SIX year is good for business, and during the year, one may more easily attract money and rewards for work. The pace must be slow but steady. It is important to be conscientious and to finish things. This may be a time when documents and contracts will require attention. There may be some behind the scenes adjustments in affairs of family and business. This is a good year for love and friendships, and is quite pleasant for home, family, and marriage. It is important to maintain a balance between home and work. The caution is to beware of worry as a lack of harmony brings about loss and disappointments.

7. *Reflect on what has taken place and how to use that information to move forward.* The SEVEN year is in some ways a sabbatical year. In the Bible it says "...and on the seventh day, God rested". This is a year to quietly withdraw and take stock of your life. This is a time for mental house-cleaning gaining greater insight and understanding in the different facets of life. During this year, one should use knowledge, resources and intuition to gain that understanding. This is a year where the concerns should be about quality, not quantity. In a SEVEN year, there will be many interesting and unusual situations and you should use reason, intellect, and intuition before implementing a course of action. In the course of this year, you may be misunderstood because of an increased level of introspection. It is important that you do not allow others to influence or alter the course you have embarked upon. This is a waiting year with no limitations. Take the time to reflect and to review past mistakes. The SEVEN year allows for introspection as a means to review past mistakes and accept them, and then to make adjustments where necessary while also analyzing the self and your projects. It is important to be truthful with yourself about your life and your desires. The SEVEN year is neither expansive nor social. It is a year for study, research, quiet time and meditation. All things should be approached with tact and diplomacy. This is the waiting period in anticipation of the upcoming EIGHT year.

8. *Accomplishment, advancement, and recognition.* The EIGHT year is a power year. With its representation of money, the EIGHT year is a year of rewards and payments for the plans and efforts put forth during the previous seven years. It is also a time to begin to think about next cycle. During the course of this year, you will haveincreased ambition and a desire to better your finances and your life. This year presents opportunities for growth and improvement and may be a year of great forward progress. There may be tests during the year and any strain they produce will be mitigated by strength, organization and efficiency. It is important that one leaves time for rest and relaxation, for if you do not, the result may be issues with your health. The EIGHT year is a year of activity, expansion, planning, thinking and acting upon the plans. This is a year of big things and opportunities. There is great promise for prosperity and success and for making contacts that will be of benefit. Be sure to delegate, so that you may concentrate on your strengths, new projects, and the accumulation of wealth. The caution is that you do not allow money to rule your life. Beware of abusing your power.

9. *Completion of plans and contemplation of new plans.* The NINE year is a year of completion, termination, and rebirth. Letting go of old, to make way for the new. Following the EIGHT year, there will also be

some rewards for this is also a year to *"reap what you have sown"*. There is more emphasis on ridding yourself of that which does not serve you, and beginning in earnest to think about the next cycle. This year is not a starting energy and therefore, you should not implement new things, projects, or relationships. Think about them, plan them, but wait for if you start them, they run a high probability of being short-lived. This is a year to tie up loose ends and clean the slate, while actively doing away with those things whose time has passed. There will be some instances where people or situations will end on their own. The NINE year is a year in which you should pay off old debts. This is a good year to increase your interest in art, culture, and music. Nines also require increased tolerance, compassion, benevolence and a more forgiving nature. Take the time to follow up on thinking of the next cycle. There is a caution to beware of impulsiveness. This may not be an easy year, because endings are sometimes uncomfortable. It is important to remember that any situations or issues that are allowed to be carried over into the next cycle will exacerbate.

11. *Be receptive to ideas and inspiration and increased recognition.* An ELEVEN year takes place in the cycle where the TWO year would appear. This is the Two year at a higher power. This is both an inner year and a year of increased public exposure and recognition. The energy of this year is geared towards spiritual growth, insight and illumination. The ELEVEN year can be quite powerful and the directive is to help others through doing good and teaching. This is a good year for finding a partner and love may appear in a "different" form. It is a time to learn to be adaptable and understanding. Flexibility is a key word. It is important to look deeply and closely at all things. The caution is to beware of negativity.

22. *Work grandly for the big(ger) picture.* A TWENTY-TWO year will fit into the cycle in place of the FOUR year, thus many of the conditions of the FOUR year are present, but in a much more powerful and practical fashion. This is a year for big projects and grand and sweeping terms of thinking. In situations where there are superiors, expect increased recognition for your efforts. The TWENTY-TWO year brings more focus on work and the affairs of life. This is a good year for travel, possibly internationally, and recognition may also result. A driving energy in this year is to do for others in big ways. The work and efforts should not be for personal gain, but must be directed outward for the good of all. From this type of direction will the rewards manifest. The cautions for this year are to beware of foolishness and folly. It is important that you know your limitations, and align with others to accomplish goals.

33. *Inspiration from a higher source towards healing and enlightenment.* A THIRTY-THREE year is a year directed towards the healing and enlighten- ment of others and self. This year is the higher vibration of the SIX year. During this time you may be extremely sensitive and should guard against negativity and opposition. In the THIRTY-THREE year, you will both attract and repel others and you should take caution in your approach to others. This is a year of a higher level of responsibility which may call for self-sacrifice and courage. It is important to maintain faith in the inner self and your principles in living life. There may be many opportunities to help others and you should discriminate in the choices that are made. Accept all responsibilities with grace and faith and have faith, that what you need will be there for you. Clues to your true purpose may be revealed during this year. Beware of martyrdom.

44. *Magnified power and accomplishments.* A FORTY-FOUR year is the higher vibration of the Eight year and is a year of great power and huge projects. A driving force here will be towards building and implementing large projects for the good of all through the use of your inner vision. This year will demand much of you and you must exhibit perseverance, resourcefulness, and caution. You will have an inner well of strength and character to face all that comes your way. It is important that you do for others, as any self-serving actions will backfire. There will be opportunities to combine the physical with the intuitive and you should develop and make use of this. A strong caution is to beware of abuses of power and tendencies towards rage and antagonism.

13

SAMPLE CHART
INTERPRETATION

CHAPTER THIRTEEN

SAMPLE CHART INTERPRETATION

	2	17/8	8	(18/9)	Soul Urge
1 1		3 59	6 1 1		
BARACK		**HUSSEIN**	**OBAMA**	19/1	Expression
2 9 3 2		8 11 5	2 4		
16/7		15/6	6	19/1	Image/Personality
9		14/5	14/5		
8		4	17/8		
		8/4/1961		20/2	Life Path
		4 4			
		0			
		0			

Challenges Inclusion Chart:

6	3	2
1	2	1
0	1	2

BARACK HUSSEIN OBAMA

SOUL URGE- 9: The NINE Soul Urge gives Barack Obama a heart energy that is compassionate, caring, philanthropic and humanitarian. He is a person who truly has concern and cares about the people he represents. It will be important for him to learn to balance the idealistic qualities of the NINE with the realities of the country he leads and the world in which he resides. His intentions are good, and when working from his heart energy, he will strive to do what is best for everyone.

IMAGE/PERSONALITY- 1: The ONE Image/Personality makes Barack Obama appear to be the one who is in charge when people meet him. His public persona is very much that of the leader, one who people can and will turn to when they are searching for answers and guidance. He is an independent thinker, and has a clear idea of who he is and what he want to accomplish.

EXPRESSION- 1: The ONE Expression amplifies and magnifies the leadership qualities of Mr. Obama. Being a leader is who he must be. His Soul Urge energy of compassion, humanitarianism, and selflessness will best manifest through his qualities of innovation and leadership. He will be a leader who has a good sense of who he is, coupled with a strong understanding of what people desire.

LIFE PATH- 20/2: Barack Obama's 20/2 Life Path shows that he is in a transitional lifetime, and that the environment where he will live and follow his course is one of allowing the energy of the Universe to work through him to accomplish the goal of bringing people together. This will come about through a desire and willingness to listen to all parties (non-partisanship) and incorporating the best ideas that people have to offer. He must learn to balance his very strong ONE energy (Soul Urge, Expression, and six Ones in the Inclusion chart) with this spirit of mediation, cooperation, and partnership.

PERSONAL YEAR- 4: Having a FOUR Personal Year (2008), means that Barack Obama is in a year where creating structure and building a strong foundation for the future is paramount. The programs and policies that are created in this year will be the foundation for the work that he does in the future. (The United States was in a THREE Personal Year when Mr. Obama was elected. This would indicate that the energy of the country would be open to creating something new through the use of the talents of the country/population.)

CHALLENGES: Mr. Obama has a FOUR challenge in the first two positions. This energy encompasses the first 43 years of his life (34 years for the first challenge, and 9 years for the second challenge). His third challenge and his lifetime challenge are both zeros. The FOUR challenge would indicate that he must be cognizant of not getting into battles over control. It is quite likely that he will either have personal control issues or will attract people that attempt to control him. His strong sense of self should diminish the severity and intensity of any such situations. Since the time frame for these challenges of FOUR is before he took office, if he learned to overcome them, they will not be an issue. The ZERO Challenge indicates that he will have many opportunities to improve any segment of his life on which he chooses to concentrate.

INCLUSION CHART:

6 - 1's

Six Ones, is double the average number of Ones found in a name. This, coupled with Obama's ONE Image and ONE Expression, gives him an extremely well-defined sense of himself. He is an innovator and natural leader, who relishes the challenges of taking charge and making things happen. On the negative side, he would have to be careful of becoming too aggressive or overbearing. This might cause him to disregard the counsel of those around him.

3 - 2's

Three Twos are also way beyond the average number of Twos one might expect to find in a name. This element of is chart provide him with a great ability to listen, digest, and comprehend opposing points of view. It also provides Obama with a degree of graciousness and charm as well as a quick wit, good sense of humor and ability to laugh at himself. The Twos in the Inclusion Chart are somewhat magnified by the fact that Mr. Obama has a TWO Life Path. This will increase the dynamic of this number in his personality.

2 - 3's

Two Threes are the high average number of Threes normally found in a name. In Mr. Obama's chart, this provides him with a gift and ability to express himself in a wonderful and warm fashion. He will connect with people on an emotional level and have the quality of making sense in that of which he speaks. Coupled with the three Twos in his chart, he is an extremely charming and self-effacing individual. This will also add a great deal of emotional energy to him, and he is likely to wear his heart on his sleeve, especially in his interpersonal relationships. This is a person who holds considerable grace and charm in his demeanor.

1 - 4

One FOUR is an average amount and this provides Mr. Obama with the ability to be organized and structured in that which he does. This, coupled with his FOUR middle cycle, allows for him to more than competently do his job and lead his country.

2 - 5's

Two Fives give Barack Obama less than the average number in his chart. The interesting dichotomy of this is that although he ran as a "candidate of change", personally he may have a difficult time with change. If he has been cognizant of this, it is possible that throughout his lifetime he has learned to embrace the change that comes into his life. In the most negative aspect of this, coupled with the overwhelming ONE energy, and the effects of the FOUR, he may be a bit dogmatic in his approach to situations and things. He must learn to temper his approach with an ability to change course and be more adaptable.

1 - 6

One SIX is an average number of occurrences in a name. This provides him with a sense of duty, responsibility, and love of family. Coupled with the Ones and FOUR energies in his chart, he is more than willing to meet the challenges and responsibilities of his life and his work.

0 - 7's

Zero Sevens is normal in charts of this period in history. It does provide the impetus to dig into the "unknowns" of life in a search of greater understanding.

1 - 8

One EIGHT, which is an average total in a name, provide Barack Obama with the ability to handle the tasks of executive leadership. This, coupled with the strong ONE energy in his chart, provides him with the qualities that it takes to handle a large undertaking.

2 - 9's

Two Nines is below the average number of Nines that an average chart would have. This would indicate that Mr. Obama needed to learn a more selfless and humanitarian approach to the people in his life. This lesson was easily mitigated by the fact that his Soul Urge is a NINE. He feels and understands the desires of the people with whom he deals.

In conclusion, Barack Obama is extremely well qualified to handle the job of President of the United States. He possesses very strong leadership qualities and qualifications, and a good balance of compassion, humanitarianism, and concern for the well-being of the people he serves. He is able to not only be a leader in principle, but also be one who can lead by example. His personal desire to serve and be of service will be a benefit in his job. His compassion and desire to make things work will be of major benefit in his quest to right the course of The United States. It is important that he continues to adequately and completely express himself and his message. His first term will be during the fourth, fifth, sixth, and seventh years of his current nine-year cycle. It is interesting to note that the next presidential election (as of the writing of this book) will be in 2012. Mr. Obama will be in his SEVEN personal year, heading into his EIGHT personal year. If he tracks the energy of this particular personal cycle, he will be gathering information to make 2012 a year of significance for him, and by extension, the country.

Pythagoras preparing for a mathematical competition with Boethius

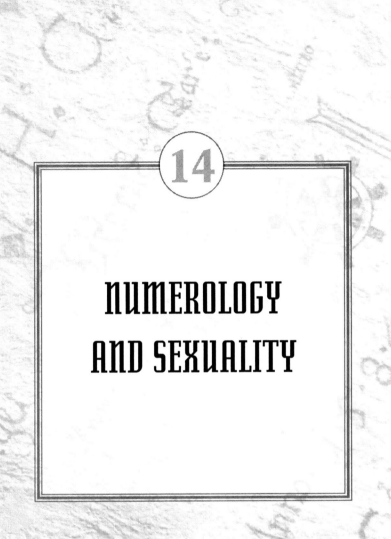

14

NUMEROLOGY AND SEXUALITY

CHAPTER FOURTEEN

NUMEROLOGY AND SEXUALITY

Numerology is an excellent tool for understanding personalities in people. Through the use and study of numbers much can be learned about the people in our lives and ourselves. Additionally, numerology can be used to determine and understand the qualities of an individual's sexual habits and drives. Since sex can be such a large part of the interaction between people, perhaps this will help to clear up some of the mystery and allow for a more freely flowing and open exchange of sexuality.

Each number contributes particular attributes and attitudes to the sexual make-up of an individual. Herewith, are the general attributes of each number. This will be followed by the attributes and attitudes attached to each number as they appear in the chart as the Soul Urge, Personality/Image, Expression, and Life Path/Birth Force.

1. "I'll do it myself!"
2. "Approach me."
3. "Let's watch them!"
4. "Let's get down to it!"
5. "Let's try it all!"
6. "I have to be in love first."
7. "Don't tell anyone, let's be sneaky."
8. "Ignore me, let's fight!"
9. "I'll think about it."

SOUL URGE

This would be the natural preference, or the direction that gives an individual the most satisfaction. This is the place of "secret desires", the fantasy world that we all have in our sexuality. Often this energy is repressed or inhibited, but when it is tapped into brings untold pleasure and delight!

1. (Masculine)-This is an aggressive tendency sexually. The ONE Soul Urge wishes to be the sexual aggressor in situations.

2. (Also 11/2) (Feminine)-This creates a subservient attitude. Someone who wants to be passive. TWOS are very receptive, submissive, gentle, and feminine. Beauty, or the perception of beauty, is also a powerful stimulant to this individual.

3. (Neither masculine or feminine)-The THREE wishes to be recognized for being a good lover. There is also an element of emotion, or emotional attachment, that is a powerful force for

the THREE Soul Urge. THREES like to watch X-rated movies, read erotic material, and enjoys any type of external i.e., third-party stimulus. The THREE also likes to laugh in bed and may indulge in immature sexual relationships.

4. (Feminine)-The FOUR tends to gravitate towards older, more mature partners as they are stimulated by the discipline of authority figures. They may enjoy a touch of S&M, as the attributes of discipline, bondage, etc., resonates within their soul. You may find that the FOUR may enjoy being tied up (or being the one who ties up) or restricted in some fashion. Since a FOUR is 2 TWOS, a FOUR Soul Urge may also have a tendency towards being very emotional.

5. (Neither masculine or feminine)-The FIVE, being a representation of the human condition and the 5 senses, tends to be very sexual and sensual. There very well may be an obsession with sex, and they are certainly curious and adventurous. FIVES like to experiment and are usually open to just about anything when it comes to sexual adventures. This is the type of individual who may have a swing or chandelier somewhere in their home, as it would provide one more place to "practice". There is a strong need for gratification, and in some instances, they may have a tendency to be a "prowler".

6. (Feminine)-This is a real lover. Love and sex have a strong link in the person with a SIX Soul Urge. This is very much a family and relationship person, and in some ways sex is not as important as it may be to other numbers. The SIX does exhibit a strong concern for their relationships and this is the bedrock upon

which their sexual tendencies is built.

7. (Neither masculine or feminine)-The SEVEN views sex from two different points...both masculine and feminine, because of this there may bebi-sexual or gay tendencies underlying their sexual drives. The natural tendency of the SEVEN is to be analytical, and they may be somewhat picky or critical of their sexual partners. The SEVEN likes unusual things, and their sexual desires may be somewhat kinky, and in some cases, perverted. The SEVEN may use sex as an escape from their everyday life or their problems. Sevens may also have a tendency to be sexual addicts, as well as having addictions to drugs, alcohol, or other stimulants or mind-altering substances and situations.

8. (Masculine)-The EIGHT, being the number of power and authority, wants to be in control. They like to take the initiative in initiating sex, and it may be a driving force within the context of their relationships. There exists a very strong sexual drive in the EIGHT and they may do whatever they feel is necessary to satisfy their sexual needs. There may be a tendency toward violence (in the most negative of situations, a rapist for instance).

9. (Neither masculine or feminine)-The NINE is usually searching for the ideal relationship and consequently the ideal sexual relationship. This condition may lead to the individual drifting in and out of relationships on a regular basis. Because NINE encompasses all of the numbers 1-8, this individual may exhibit some or all of the tendencies of the other numbers at any given time.

PERSONALITY/IMAGE

This would be the individual's instinctive reaction to sex and sexual situations. This number also shows how others would view the individual, although that perception may not be grounded in any reality of the person being viewed. If an individual is not in touch with their fantasy side (Soul Urge) this may be the dominant characteristic sexually.

1. (Masculine) - The ONE Personality would be assumed to be aggressive by others.

2. (Feminine) - The TWO would appear to be feminine and receptive to the overtures of love and sex.

3. (Neither masculine or feminine) - The THREE would appear to like younger partners to match their own emotional level. They like to joke around and have fun in bed, but they would expect you to laugh with them.

4. (Feminine) - FOURs appear to have control and they tend to be the teacher, correcting as they proceed. There may be a tendency to be somewhat boring in bed, and might like to "let's go and get it over with!"

5. (Neither masculine or feminine) - FIVEs appear very sexual and may be somewhat of a teaser. They are very attractive and usually well dressed. They can be very stimulating to others, and at times may be unaware that they are attractive to others.

6. (Feminine) - Here again, the SIX appears to be more interested in the relationship aspect. They appear "motherly" (whether male or female) and may attract individuals who are looking to be "taken care of".

7. (Neither masculine or feminine)-The SEVEN may attract others because they are seen as different and somewhat strange in their sexual habits. This individual may be somewhat out of the ordinary, and may appear aloof to others. Their approach to sexuality may take on somewhat of an intellectual approach. They may also be somewhat inhibited or repressed.

8. (Masculine)-The EIGHT Personality/Image appears very sexual with a very strong sex drive. Their vibration of power and domination may attract individuals who are looking to be submissive sexually, and could lead to situations that may be somewhat abusive.

9. (Neither masculine or feminine)-The NINE exhibits patience in all situations. They may appear carefree and unattached. This attitude may attract individuals who are not looking for something other than a good time. Almost a "love 'em and leave 'em" attitude.

EXPRESSION

The Expression constitutes the ultimate attitude of an individual sexually. The fully integrated person will be comfortable with their sexuality and will readily exhibit their true sexual nature as demonstrated by their Soul Urge.

To truly understand how this will manifest, read the Soul Urge and Personality/Image number in relation to the Life Path/Birth Force number, as well as the Inclusion Table (the Karmic Lessons) for numbers that are missing in an individual's name. This interpretation will give you a very clear-cut idea of the sexuality of the person you are charting.

1. (Masculine)- The ONE is most comfortable when they have full control of their sexual situations and when they are being aggressive. They wish to take charge and be the "director" and will perform best when placed in this situation.

2. (Feminine)- The TWO is most comfortable in the submissive role as this is instinctively what they choose to be. Since beauty and sensuality are so important to the TWO, they appreciate being told what to do in a loving and caring fashion. They will respond to the dominant partner and enjoy it.

3. (Neither masculine or feminine)- There is a part of the THREE that needs no partner, they will gladly do it themselves as they can be very strongly stimulated by external images (movies, books, voyeurism, etc.) The THREE has a wonderfully fantastic imagination and has the ability to use it in a very fulfilling manner.

4. (Feminine)- The FOUR may have a somewhat selfish attitude towards sex, and are quite likely wishing to "do it and get it over with". They can be very disciplined in their approach and may take a somewhat mechanical, boring approach to their sexual adventures.

5. (Neither masculine or feminine)- The FIVE may possess

restlessness with regards to sex. They get bored easily, and are constantly looking for new and additional stimulation. They derive a great deal of pleasure from indulging in pleasures of the senses and have a real talent for sex. This quality can lead to a gigolo/hooker type of mentality.

6. (Feminine)- This is the sentimental, romantic number in numerology. The romance of sex is very important to the SIX, and they tend to be very loyal in their relationships. They are quite content to be with one person, as long as they are happy. They may have a martyr quality when it comes to their families, and the SIX possesses a very straightforward attitude to sex and relationships.

7. (Neither masculine or feminine)- There is an out of the ordinary, unconventional attitude to sex that belongs to the SEVEN They enjoy unusual relationships, and may have a tendency towards bi-sexual or gay couplings. At the least, there may be a tendency to be bi-curious. Sevens can possess addictive tendencies (drugs, alcohol, etc.) and it may have an effect on how they like to perform sexually, i.e., under the influence. They do have a willingness to indulge in kinky sexual behavior, and in a healthy sexual environment can be quite a bit of fun.

8. (Masculine)- The EIGHT desires to have their entire life under some sort of control, and sex is no exception to this. They may use sex to get what they want from someone, and at times may appear to have no romantic inclinations at all.

9. (Neither masculine or feminine)- The humanitarian and

philanthropic nature of the NINE shines through in their sexual relationships also. They are "givers" and will participate even if they are not in the mood, out of a desire to maintain harmony and to fulfill the wishes of another.

THE LIFE PATH/BIRTH FORCE or DAY OF BIRTH

This number (either the Life Path or Day of Birth) will provide an indication of whom you are destined to wind up with. The greatest compatibility is shown when the Life Path and Soul Urge numbers are the same, i.e. one person's Soul Urge is the same as their partners Life Path, and vice versa.

1. This person is more interested with receiving sex and sexual pleasure than giving it. Their tendency would be to draw to themselves selfish and inconsiderate partners.

2. This is a person who wants to be approached. Love is very important to them and eye contact is a must.

3. The person with a THREE Life Path or Day of Birth needs to express himself or herself, and will be receptive to being asked to do so. They wish to feel young and want their egos massaged. They like to hear stories and may have a tendency towards being flashers or exhibitionists.

4. This individual may take a very disciplined approach to their sexual activities, almost wanting to have a schedule. Their approach may be very serious, and they don't like much foreplay. Restriction, bondage, whips, chains and the like may turn

them on. They may love to have sex in a vehicle.

5. The FIVE Life Path or Day of Birth likes unusual partners and may not seem choosy, although they are turned on by physical appearance. This turn-on will be in the "eyes of the beholder," but their partners will tend to have some overriding, appealing physical characteristic(s). There may be a free-spirited approach to their sexual activities and they may not have a desire to stay with anyone for an extended period of time. Many times, they have no real desire for a relationship, preferring a series of sexual partners. They may also have a proclivity for extreme behavior.

6. The SIX wishes to be the "Cosmic Mother" and this will lead to an overwhelming desire to please their partner. They love oral sex, hugging and kissing. The SIX is a real lover and will exhibit behavior in line with this desire.

7. This individual may have a tendency to be very secretive; on the negative they will be downright sneaky. The SEVEN is always looking for their ideal mate. They may exhibit hypochondriac tendencies or be visiting doctors and hospitals regularly. They don't share their feelings unless they truly want to, and when they do it will be on their terms. There may also appear to be a very reserved quality to this person. They may have a tendency to look at other people as though there is something wrong with them. They expect maturity and sophistication from others.

8. The easiest way to attract a person with an EIGHT Life Path or Day of Birth may be to ignore them. There may be some "crazy" tendencies in their personality or approach to sexual

relations and they can be quite impulsive. This impulsiveness may make it difficult to make dates with them. Sexually, they will perform their sexual acts wherever they can and will use sex to get what they desire (on the negative side, this may lead to being a hooker or gigolo). Sex may not be as important as what they can get from it. There may be a tendency for "business first".

9. The NINE is ultimately looking for the ideal lover/sexual partner and may only wish to have sex if they can be "enlightened" by something. There may be a very strong desire to please their partner or to play a role, if they believe that is what their partner is looking for.

In closing, you must look closely at a person's entire chart before applying the tendencies addressed in this chapter. By analyzing the confluence of the different numbers, you will be able to get a clear picture of the type of sexual being an individual is and this can be used to enhance the lovemaking aspect of your relationships. Any over-abundance of a particular number in the Inclusion Chart will amplify and magnify the tendencies that are listed in each section.

KARMIC LESSONS

These are the numbers that are missing in the spelling of the name. These numbers that are missing will impact, and have an influence on, the conditions that are listed in the previous section, i.e. Soul Urge, Personality/Image, and Expression, when it comes to the sexual tendencies.

Missing 1's- This individual will have problems with being aggressive due to a lack of confidence leading to a person who may be subservient and insincere.

Missing 2's- This individual may not know how to be passive or feminine, and may have trouble relating to women. In men, it may cause a degree of insensitivity.

Missing 3's- This exacerbates intimate relationships as it causes an inability to express. This individual may attempt to overcompensate sexually to make up for the inability to express.

Missing 4's- This lack of FOUR may lessen the structured approach and rigidity of the individual. It may actually be a blessing, as it will loosen up the person.

Missing 5's- Sex is no big deal to this individual, they don't really need it, but they will be very concerned with giving others pleasure. If the individual has an overabundance of Fives (4 or more) they will express highly repeated demand, almost insatiable.

Missing 6's-Without the constraints of the energy of "responsibility" this person will have a tendency to want to "let loose" and a willingness to try kinky things.

Missing 7's- Although this individual may not admit it, they are searching for a sexual outlet or release.

Missing 8's- The individual who is missing the number EIGHT in the spelling of their name would not come on as strongly as one who has Eights in their name. This may temper the sexual energy of someone who has a strong Eight vibration in his or her major numbers (Soul Urge, etc.)

Missing 9's- The one who is missing Nines in their name will come across as insensitive and selfish, giving no or little regard to their partners desires.

15

HOUSE
NUMBERS

CHAPTER FIFTEEN

HOUSE NUMBERS

To determine the numerological vibration of the house, use the house number as it appears on the house e.g., 336, 25, 148, etc. Total the digits and reduce to a single number, unless of course, it is an 11, 22, 33, 44, 55, 66, 77, 88, or 99. If the home is an apartment, use the mailing address number for the overall energy, and then the apartment number for the particular energy e.g. 3D, 168F, etc.

1- This is a good vibration if someone is living by themselves. ONE represents extreme independence and will support the individual in their life. If this is an apartment the individual may receive little or no help.

COLOR: Red (and shades of red) is best

TROUBLE: Roof and ceiling

2- This creates a sensitive and quiet environment. A good place for couples or partners. Collectors will find this vibration conducive for collecting.

146 • MICHAEL JOHN FIERRO

There may be TWOs of many things.

> COLOR: Orange (and shades of orange) is best
> TROUBLE: Windows, doors, & floors.

3- This is a social and friendly vibration. Conversations, parties, happiness, music, and creative talents are emphasized. This is a home of constantly ringing phones. This is a good environment for children.

> COLOR: Yellow (and shades of yellow) is best.
> TROUBLE: Cracks, insulation, & major appliances.

4- FOUR is a good work environment. Vibrationally it creates a disciplined and organized environment. Work may be a constant presence and the energy may be somewhat restrictive. Throw rugs and many plants should be part of the decorating scheme.

> COLOR: Green (and shades of green) is best.
> TROUBLE: Cracks, leaks, doors, & windows. Pay special attention to things of a structural nature (foundation, etc).

5- This is a high-level energy environment. There may be constant movement of furniture and continual changes. There will be much moving in and out, talk of travel and adventure, cars and sex. A nervous energy may be present.

> COLOR: Lighter blues and turquoise.
> TROUBLE: Electrical problems and appliances.

6- This is the consummate "home" energy. A good number for raising family and engaging in family activities. Cooking, gardening and other home activities may be prevalent. This is a home that may very well have a dog, and that may attract dogs from the neighborhood. It will also attract neighbors and friends. There will be an assortment of different things throughout the home.

> COLOR: Darker blues.
> TROUBLE: May be centered in the kitchen and family areas.

7- The SEVEN home will be one of introspection, research, reading, investigations, and spiritual pursuits. It is not a social environment. It is a vibration that may be conducive to drinking, drugs, perversions, and depression.

> COLOR: Indigo, pink, purple.
> TROUBLE: Water and plumbing and anything to do
> with water.

8- EIGHT creates a good environment for a home-based business. It may create money pressures and worries for the inhabitants. Fights, noise and upset may be frequent. This can be an impressive home, but should not be so for the purpose of "keeping up with the Joneses" or ego-centered impressing of others.

> COLOR: Deep purples, gold, and red.
> TROUBLE: Plumbing, bathrooms, bug and insect
> infestations, fires.

9-The NINE home "belongs to the world". It is an environment of the open house. It will attract many people and in some instances it will attract problems. The NINE home may create health problems for the inhabitants.

> COLOR: All colors and color combinations.
> TROUBLE: Since NINE encompasses all numbers, all
> the problems of the other numbers may be a
> factor. Also, health of the occupants.

16

UNDERSTANDING YOURSELF (AND OTHERS)

CHAPTER SIXTEEN

UNDERSTANDING YOURSELF (AND OTHERS)

In conclusion, Numerology provides an insightful means to understand yourself and the people who surround you. A comprehensive analysis reveals information about every aspect of personality, way of doing things, conditions that may create situations where someone acts up, or acts out, and even sexuality. Through the use of Numerology, one can better understand the significant people in their lives. It can also be used in business to better understand your employees, employers, business partners and potential clients and customers.

The number of the Soul Urge provide you with the "heart of hearts" energy, the true driving force in someone's life. It is this number which represents where a person's life will be most content and "real". This is the spirit/being portion of someone. SPIRIT.

The Image/Personality number is the means in which the Soul Urge number will "come to life". This is the thinking part of a person. One must learn to find the way to best use this energy to manifest that which the heart desires. This is the doing/ego portion of someone. MIND.

The Expression is the sum of the parts ie, the Soul Urge and the Image/Personality. This is who the individual must "be" in this lifetime and is the ultimate result of the manifestation of the Soul Urge through the Image/Personality. A truly balanced person will discover the way to live that will honor both their "being" with their "doing/ego". BODY.

In the spelling of the name is the BODY/MIND/SPIRIT trinity that is every living person. This is the "car in life that you are driving", as just as you would familiarize yourself with the Owner's Manual that comes with a new car, it is important that you become familiar with the Owner's Manual that is your name.

The Life Path is the world or environment in which you will get to exercise who you are as denoted by your name. This is the field of experience of the material world. If your name is the "car in life that you are driving", the Life Path is the "road in life that you are traveling". This is the energy that supports who you are, and as any road may have, there are potholes and obstacles. These are represented by the Challenges. These "obstacles to wholeness" are the major issues of life and it is important that the individual identifies and works with them. When a Challenge is overcome, it becomes a tool for living a fuller life of improved circumstances. The lesson with the Challenges is that "...when you overcome them, you become them", and it is at this point that they become an enhancement.

Particular attention should be paid to the Inclusion chart, for this part of a numerological interpretation alerts you to the personality of someone.

It also represents the lessons of life, and the areas in the personality on which focus must be placed. If an Inclusion chart is viewed as a tool-belt, then the missing numbers are the tools that must be acquired. If a number is below average in the number of times it appears, then the tool is there but it must be improved upon. An overabundance of any particular number will produce an extreme in personality or behavior. Through the interpretation and analysis of the Inclusion chart in conjunction with the main numbers of the name, a thorough and insightful understanding of someone will be achieved.

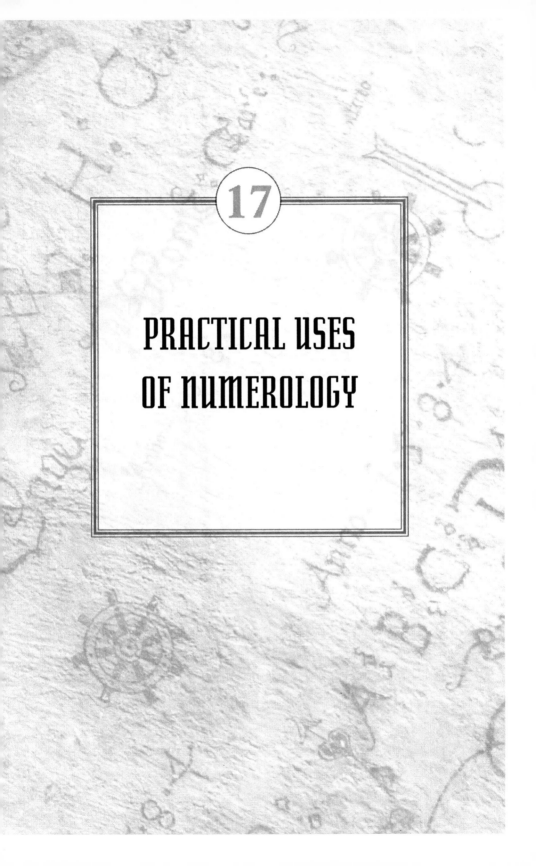

17

PRACTICAL USES
OF NUMEROLOGY

CHAPTER SEVENTEEN

PRACTICAL USES OF NUMEROLOGY

As a final note, here is a list of ways in which numerology may be used to assist in life and business situations. As you become more familiar in working with numerology, you will find ways to make use of the insights and information that can be obtained through an analysis.

1. Self-awareness and understanding including intrapersonal relationships brought about by a name change.

2. Interpersonal relationships between a couple, or a family situation.

3. Business relationships where an understanding of business partners and/or potential clients or associations would be necessary or beneficial.

4. As a tool in the realm of education, so teachers, counselors, and administrators may better understand the children they are teaching and molding.

5. Understanding the cycles of life and the influences that are at play and using these cycles to maximize individual projects and efforts.

6. Understanding the timing of events, and taking that information to use to your advantage to again maximize individual projects and efforts.

7. To determine conducive and supportive colors to be chosen in the home and in choosing clothing to maximize the vibrational effect and presentation.

8. Names and colors for business enterprises (logo, trade name, etc.) so the business is vibrationally presented at its ultimate effect.

Ancient numerological scroll

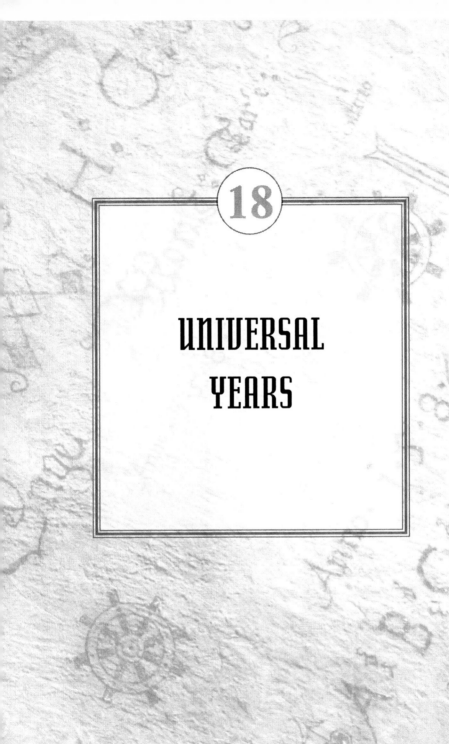

18

UNIVERSAL YEARS

CHAPTER EIGHTEEN

UNIVERSAL YEARS

2009 - Universal Year • A Look Back

Numerology follows a repetitive pattern of the numbers one through nine. Just as in a personal chart which has personal year and cycles, so too, are their Universal years and cycles. These cycles continually proceed through time and they represent a nine-year period. This period should be looked at collectively, with each year being a step along the way, and each succeeding year building upon the previous one. Universal years have an effect on the entire planet as a general vibration that has influence on everyone and everything. A Universal year will provide an indication of what types of trends and things may occur in the world, while the people of the world may be unaware of its effect. This vibration influences that in which people may become interested and what types of events may happen.

In this chapter, I present essays on the Universal years ELEVEN (2) through FIVE, covering the period of time from 2009-2012. These essays will describe the conditions and events that are indicated by the ruling numerological vibrations of the year. In calculating the Universal year, one should add all four digits of the year and then reduce the total to a single digit (unless the total is a Master Number such as ELEVEN or TWENTY-TWO).

EXAMPLES:

2010 (2+0+1+0=3)

2009 (2+0+0+9=11)

1995 (1+9+9+5=24=6)

1984 (1+9+8+4=22)

1955 (1+9+5+5=20=2)

In the twentieth century, the world experienced two ELEVEN Universal years (1901 and 1910) and seven TWENTY-TWO Universal years (1939, 1948, 1957, 1966, 1975, 1984 and 1993). During the 21st century we will experience an ELEVEN Universal year every nine years beginning with 2009 for the firstpart of the century. There will be no TWENTY-TWO Universal year during the lifetime of anyone reading this book.

Numerologically, 2009 was an ELEVEN universal year and the 2nd year in the 9-year cycle. In numerology, one measure of life is in series of 9-year periods. These 9-year periods are constantly repeated. A way to look at a cycle is to think of a garden. In a 1-year, you would plan and plant your garden. Each succeeding year, you would tend to that garden accordingly and as long as you followed the proper steps and procedures, in the 8th and 9th years, you would reap what you have sown.

2008 was the first year in this particular cycle. It ushered in a period of change and transformation that may reach a pinnacle on December 21,

2012 (the generally accepted time of the end of the Mayan calendar). In some regards, 2008 was the beginning of the end in the sense that things, e.g. civilization, establishments, government, etc, began changing. We have already witnessed the breakdown of the financial systems, the beginnings of massive changes in the industrial/corporate world, and in the geopolitical vein, a new and progressive time. This is not to imply that things will suddenly become better and more fair for citizens of not only the United State, but the world. What it does portend is that the systems as we know them, ae collapsing under the weight of their own excesses and inequities. In my opinion, things as we know them, must be deconstructed so they may be rebuilt.

The ELEVEN energy of 2009 brought about both positive and negative changes on a global scale. I will address the negative energies first to point out the pitfalls that had an effect on the future and how we need to collectively get involved in bringing about positive, long-lasting, and all-encompassing changes. In numerology, ELEVEN is what is known as a master number. These are numbers of increased spirituality and higher calling. Master numbers are the leaders for change and improvements in consciousness and living. Eleven is the intuitive and inspirational leader, the teacher of the higher good. All master numbers, if not exercised on the higher plane, revert to the worst characteristics of the lower number. In this case, the lower number is 2 and when elevens are manifested on the two level, it creates a situation of complacency, loss of belief and faith, and the energy of "doormat", i.e. being taken advantage of, manipulated, and abused.

On the national and global stage 2009 included a rise in crime of all types, that is corporate and civil. As the economic situation deteriorated, people were inclined to take what they needed. To guard against the continuation of this activity, we must all, in the future, learn to be compassionate, benevolent, and philanthropic. This is a time that begs for people to return to a sense of community and neighborhoods. If you wish to become involved in a community movement, go to *www.relocalize.net* and learn about the growing local movement that is happening worldwide.

2009 also saw a rise in impulsiveness, smugness, fanaticism, and indifference on the part of leaders. The caution here would have been to think before acting on a personal level. On a global level, it is important that people become involved in holding our leaders (both governments and business) accountable. If the current economic situation continues on its current course, more and more people will become affected. Shortages of supplies and interruptions in services may create events where people REACT, without thinking things through. Again, the caution is to behave from a global and community perspective. Accountability applies to everyone, citizens and leaders alike. Collectively, change may be brought about through right words, right actions, and right beliefs. Make sure our voices are heard and that "we the people" are again made a part of the decision-making process. The negative aspect of the ELEVEN energy made people nervous, flighty, and prone to poor decisions. We needed to think, and more importantly, FEEL the rightness of words and actions before moving forward. Social unrest and upheaval certainly resulted from wrong-minded behavior.

There was also an increase in legal activities around money. People seeking redress for the loss of their savings, pensions, benefits, etc. Many of those who manipulated and abused the system(s) were held accountable.

On the positive side 2009 lead to a global tendency towards spirituality, inner development, reverence and highest honesty and illumination. This is a trend that has become more important and popular over the previous years, and 2009 amplified that activity. People and countries became more in tune with their own identities. This marginally lead to a greater interest in idealistic thought and action, as well as the spreading of ideas and an expounding of beliefs. The caution would have been, is that which is mentioned in a previous paragraph, to avoid a tendency towards fanaticism. Individuals and countries must be governed by idealism and inspiration. The concept of "the common good" must once again be a hallmark of people and societies.

We must encourage and embrace greater philanthropic and altruistic tendencies. We must stand up for ourselves, as individuals and societies, to bring about change that makes life good and equitable for ALL. We must learn to worship and revere all that is good in life and hold everyone, especially ourself, to a higher standard of existence and co-existence.

2009 brought about a greater interest and pursuit in matters of spirit and spirituality. Religions showed some change and adjustment to better meet the needs and desires of their members. Collectively, movement needed to be made towards the "oneness" of all there is. Greater interest and progress in educational pursuits may also come about resulting in a better informed, more enlightened populace. This will assist in wiping out the ignorance of self-centered, greedy behavior on the part of governments, businesses, and most importantly...individuals. Sudden events will demand decisive action and decisive action is best implemented by those who are aware and educated.

In tarot, the ELEVEN represents JUSTICE and 2009 demanded balance through justice. We needed to become aware of the nuances of cause and effect to create action of a positive, enlightening, and benevolent nature. As with every decision and turning point in life, we always have two choices that we can make. These choices are dictated by the only two, real forces that exist...LOVE and FEAR. Remember that fear defeats love, and love defeats fear. Raise yourself, and by extension, your community and the world through right action, positive thought, and outpouring of love and understanding. The course which was chosen in 2009 had a MAJOR impact on the direction the world will take in the following years. As we move towards December 21, 2012 (an ELEVEN day in a FIVE universal year, i.e. a year of transition and change) it is important that we remain aware of the consequences and outcomes of our daily decisions and actions.

I implore all who are reading this to go deep within and find the absolute core of goodness and light that resides inside each of us. Connect with that place and carry it forth into the world. Become more locally and community-minded. By positively impacting the micro, we will be able to bring about the positive change in the macro.

2010 - 3 Universal Year

umerologically, the year 2010 is a THREE Universal year (2+0+1+0=3). In numerology, THREE represents creation, creative self-expression, emotion, artistic talents and endeavors, and healing and the healing arts.

2010 may turn out to be a pivotal year worldwide, as the positives and negatives are quite diametrically opposed and dramatic, and the emotional quotient that will be at play may bring about situations of an extreme nature. On the positive side, 2010 has already shown to be a fertile ground for an expansion in the world of arts, entertainment, and recreation. Properly used, this energy will be conducive for the production of artistic works that can have a beneficial effect on those who are exposed to them. The climate will encourage the expression of thoughts, ideas and emotions and will also be a platform for social issues and interactions. The THREE, being the number of creation, may also be a driving force in a continuation of spiritual understanding that was begun in 2009, an ELEVEN Universal year. (See my previous entry on the meaning of 2009). This would be a good year to begin in earnest, the healing of the Self and the planet on which we reside. 2010 can be the birth of something new. All such progress and ideas must begin with the individual and the energy will be such, that progress and ideas may be carried forth into the collective. People will definitely be more inclined to search for answers.

In the tarot, the number THREE is The Empress, who represents the subconscious mind. Here, the response to our memories can create growth through imagination. This energy is the epitome of creation and abundance as represented by Venus. Revelations 12:1-2 says, "And there appeared a great wonder in heaven; a woman clothed with the sun, and the moon under her feet, and upon her head a crown of twelve stars; And she being with child cried, travailing in birth, and pained to be delivered."* We can give birth to a new consciousness, a new way of existing, a new way of co-existing. The dangers of the excesses which are such a part of the fabric of our world today, must be acknowledged and abolished. We must create that which is fair and just to all for the negative side of the THREE Universal year is not pleasant and may create more imbalance, unfairness and dis-ease upon us and our planet.

Astrologically, the number THREE is associated with the planet Jupiter. In Indian numerology and astrology, Jupiter is the remover of darkness and a teacher of righteousness, justice and self-illumination. We must continue to shed the darkness and move towards the light. The journey and the lifting of the veil begins with each of us as individuals. As within, so without. As above, so below.

What remains of 2010 should bring about new developments in the world of medicine and pharmaceuticals. I would anticipate a major breakthrough in the treatment, and/or elimination, of at least one major health affliction. This may also be a year in which words take on a new level of importance. We, the people, may find a new voice through which we can express our dissatisfaction and upsets with the powers that be. It may be a multitude of individuals or it may be the voice of a new leader, or leaders, who may galvanize people into action. Watch for a major talk or speech by a world leader that will have tremendous effect on all. There may also be new "words" regarding justice and law and order. On the positive side, this may be a new approach to the way crimes and criminals are handled. Negatively, it may portend new laws that may be more restrictive (especially in matters of speech and self-expression). This could lead to crackdowns on the voice of dissension around the globe.

As people look to create more recreation and fun activities in their lives, we may see the introduction of some new, fun-based or recreational fad. There may also be a collective lifting of spirits through the spending of more money on fun and leisure activities. The inclination will be for people to enjoy life, and the fears and obstacles of the current economic situations may be dissipated through a collective desire to break loose and throw caution to the wind.

The negative side of the THREE Universal year may be quite dramatic as there may be a tendency towards extreme emotional reactions, and even overreactions, to events. Such activities could lead to more oppressive behavior and actions from those in power. Every action creates an equal reaction. With that in mind, caution must be exercised and be preceded by thoughtful contemplation. People must also be aware of a tendency to scatter energy. Attempting too much, too quickly will not produce anything that is worthwhile. Restlessness and recklessness are certainly conditions of which people are mindful. This applies not only to individuals, but governments as well. Such behaviors will create greater tensions between the parties involved. (Watch for this to manifest between countries in the global arena.) There may be an increase in the use of guns and weapons, and an escalation in brutality and aggressive or warlike behavior.

Even more importantly, people, institutions and governments must be aware of the fact that extreme actions and behaviors will create equally great and extreme results and reactions. Extravagance will lead to a dissipation of wealth and resources; an exhaustion of resources will lead to a wasteland; and risk will lead to more loss. The indication here would be that the lessons of the past two years have not been learned, and we will all suffer accordingly. The lesson here is to avoid excess. Be conservative and resourceful.

The more that pleasure is pursued, the more likely the result will be less constructive outcomes. To illustrate this, think back to what the excesses of 1929 led to...the crash of 1929 and the world was plunged into its worst ever economic crisis. The situations of 1938 led to the outbreak of World War II. The peace that followed WWII (1947) led to the Atomic Age and the beginning of the Cold War. The tensions of the Cold War in 1956 led to an increase in the race for technological advantages and an escalation in the geo-political climate in the world. 1965 was the harbinger of social changes never before seen. 1974 saw a political scandal and tragedy of new proportions, and the world was never the same. 1983 saw dramatic situations in the economic climate. 1992 brought with it a new level of partisanship and divisiveness in the political arena. 2001 brought us the events of September 11, and a new level of government interference and the erosion of personal liberties and rights. A new dynamic was created. The common thread here is the fact that all of the years mentioned were THREE Universal years. Be mindful that more greed and wasteful extravagance will precede trouble. Watch for the dramatic event(s) in 2010 and know that another shift is upon us. It is this very energy which we must collectively work to change.

Through positive creation and actions and activities of an enlightened nature, the outcomes can be affected. We must use our voices and speak out against the injustices, excesses, and abuses of which we become aware. We are one year closer to the end of the 4th age as predicted by the indigenous people around the world. The ride may get bumpier, but the potential for a new and better world is always there for the creating. Be true to yourself. Use the creative energy of 2010, and make the changes which will benefit your immediate world, and the world as a whole.

My thanks to Dusty Bunker for this insight.

2011- 4 Universal Year

2011 is the 4th year in the current Universal nine-year cycle. As with all years, there are positive and negative aspects, and it is my belief, considering the current worldwide situation that once again, there may be extremes on both sides. Much will be determined by the actions and activities of the preceding year, 2010 (a THREE Universal year).

On the positive side, 2011 can be a year of concrete action directed towards creating and building a more stable world for the future. Certain aspects of the FOUR represent structure, foundations, and organization. This year has potential to be a ground-breaking year in the re-creation of a world that accommodates and cares for everyone. When one considers the breakdown of systems and establishments in the preceding three years, it can be understood how these systems must be rebuilt, and how they must be reconstructed to benefit the many, and not the few. This should be a year of slow and careful building resulting in permanent and useful terms.

2011 should see an increase in construction projects and in government projects related to infrastructure and commerce. There may be a reversal in the recent defense spending decreases, as governments look to bolster their national security. There may be a renewed interest and participation in farming, both on a large scale and in an increased interest in home gardens. A portion of this interest will emanate from a greater desire by people to exercise thrift and economy in their personal lives. The FOUR vibration is also beneficial for the sectors concerning manufacturing and education.

Another positive aspect of a FOUR Universal year is a greater desire toward tact and cooperation between people; citizenry and their governments; and between countries on a global scale. There may be a challenge to traditions and recently accepted modes of behavior. This has great potential to reestablish the bond between governments and their citizens on a more cooperative and equitable level.

Economically, 1930 was a FOUR Universal year and we may experience similar situations in the rebuilding of the economy. As jobs slowly reappear, we may find that wages are not at the level they were previously. This may be a necessity as countries and corporations, around the globe work to reestablish a more stable environment. Special attention must be paid to the negative aspects of the FOUR vibration of 2011, as much of this will be determined by how current situations are handled by those in power. 2011 may see a rise in violence and violent confrontations. This rise may be in the form of civil disobedience and/or wars. How governments and power entities react to people raising their voices will have a great effect on the behavior of those people. Dissension, and a move away from conventional behavior(s) may be the result of people's dissatisfaction with their leaders. On the most extreme level, reactions by leaders and governments could range from crackdowns, police and/or military actions, and even martial law being established. The 4 represents restrictions, confinement, obstacles and prison. Societies may exercise a greater level of offensive behavior dissension may be expressed. Were situations to escalate, people may be surprised at the level of reaction that is exercised.

On the economic front, there may be a shortage of liquidity in business, government, and on a personal level. This would be a direct result of the excesses of the "good times" and the failure of individuals, nations and corporate entities to realize the errors of their ways. Just as Icarus flew too close to the sun and crashed back to earth, so may the economy find that it too "flew too high only to fall hard, back to reality". Hard times may become a reality for many. If too many people become accustomed to not working or living on hand-outs, there may be a decrease in incentive to work and laziness may become an all-too-familiar trait.

As with all vibrations in numerology (and all situations in life), choices must be made on an individual and collective level. The negative aspects of 2011 should be impetus enough for people to work towards making this a better world in which to live. Check your history and look back at the changes that were fomented in 1966 (a 22/4 Universal year)...a year in which the structure of society was torn down and the beginning of a rebuilding took place. The world is changing. As can be seen by the events and situations yearly since 2008 (a ONE Universal year), nothing is immune to changes and transformations. You, the individual, must work toward bettering your personal existence and by doing that, you can help to change the collective. Be aware of your behavior, beliefs, and mind-set and pay attention to that which is going on in the world around you. Take part in making your voice heard in creating fairness and equity for all.

2012- 5 Universal Year

There may be no year, in all of history that has elicited as much dialogue, literature and discussion as 2012. Most people are aware of 2012's association with the end of the Mayan calendar, which takes place on December 21, 2012. I will not go into the deeper, esoteric meaning of the date in this book. From the perspective of numerology, 2012 is a FIVE Universal year. A FIVE year is a year of change, transformation, transitions, and movement. It is also a representation of the human condition (the 5 senses). With that in mind, 2012 portends a culmination of the changes that have been sweeping the planet over the past few years. This year has the potential to finally place humankind on a new and more beneficial (to all) course. As with all years, there are positive and negative aspects that must be considered.

The positive aspects of a FIVE Universal year indicate an increase in the activity surrounding commerce and trade, with an improvement in the overall economic conditions globally. This may be the year when the world financial picture shows some sustained growth with a healthier outlook. This, of course, will be directly effected by the groundwork and foundation that is laid in 2011.

More important in the context of the FIVE year will be conditions and situations concerning the human condition. 2012 should see a great increase in the interest in metaphysics and psychology...a more intense and far-reaching desire to more fully understand our existence here on Earth. In numerology, FIVE is an indication of the human experience and the FIVE senses, and it is within this context where a greater focus will be aimed. People will be drawn to better educating themselves in new and different subjects, while simultaneously intensifying their knowledge of the "whys" of their lives. There will be a development in new attitudes and beliefs, and a rejuvenation of the human spirit. A rise in the condition of the "one" will be seen as a natural baseline for the rising up of all of mankind. Individuals will look to not only gain deeper insight and understanding into their personal existence, they will also be more in-tune with their part in the bigger picture..." what part do I play in the whole?" People will be much more aware of the effects that their individual efforts have on the collective. We may see an increase in heroic actions that lift us all to a better place. This may all be coupled with new and (in the context of the times) radical views on the way we live and co-exist with one another and our planet. The FIVE Universal year brings about expansion in many realms of living. There will be an undercurrent of change and transition that will affect societies and the way things are handled (think back to the social changes of 1967). People will more fully understand the importance of being versatile and of possessing the innate ability to foster the changes necessary to improve the "race consciousness" as it pertains to living in concert with the planet on which we reside. Improvements in many aspects of living and commerce may be brought about. New ideas and thought patterns that more keenly connect us to our sense of spirit and our thoughts about oneness may spring up in all segments, cultures, and countries around the globe.

On the negative side of the 5 Universal year, there may be an increase in international nervousness, as reactions to the impending changes are met with fear and a show of force. One of the other conditions the 5 represents are the tenets of law and order. While people will be seeking justice, the powers that be may react by using new, and more restrictive laws to hold onto their place of power. As the old way of doing things falls away, we may experience great opposition to the new, more radical thoughts and beliefs that will permeate the mindset of people. Political assassinations may take place, as people looking to foster change, but who are working out of fear, may feel it necessary to make an urgent and dramatic statement.

One of the key conditions of the number 5 is BALANCE. It is of the utmost importance, that everyone seeks, and discovers, their own personal middle ground. One must understand, and take responsibility for their actions while giving thought to the effect their actions may have on the overall picture. One of the schools of thought associated with December 21, 2012 is it is the end of the 4th age, as understood by indigenous cultures around the world. The 5th age is the age of man. We are moving into a time where we will once again, more greatly understand our connection to one another, and to Mother Earth. If a positive outlook and belief system can take root, we will all get to experience a better life and existence. In many ways, this will be a time of rebirth... rebirth of balance, harmony, joy, compassion, consideration and love. It is this author's prayer that you gain the understanding and insight, so you may get to enjoy that which lies before you. Namaste. Blessings of love and light.

Numerology is everywhere

1. U.S. 1 Highway sign. 2. The IRT #2 train. 3. Babe Ruth. 4. Old sign Okracoke, NC 1978. 5. Charles Demuth (1883-1935) The Figure 5 in Gold (1928) Alfred Stieglitz Collection Metropolitan Museum of Art. 6. Playing cards. 7. Old 7up sign somewhere on the road to Florida 1984. 8. 8 ball. 9. Old neon clock in a diner on the Pennsylvania Turnpike, 1981. *Photos ©Gregg Hinlicky 2010*

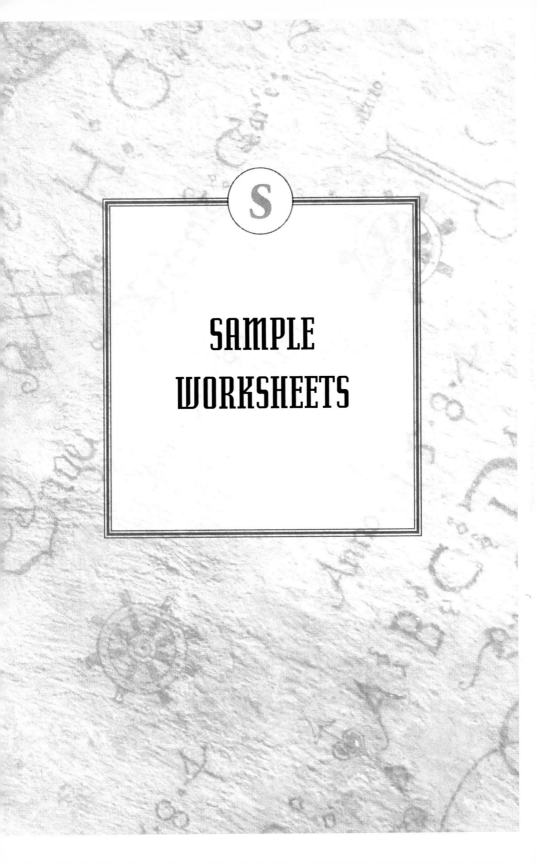

SAMPLE
WORKSHEETS

SAMPLE WORKSHEET

This is an example of the format that you should use when constructing a chart. Again, be certain that you allow yourself enough room above, and below the name and birth date to do your calculations.

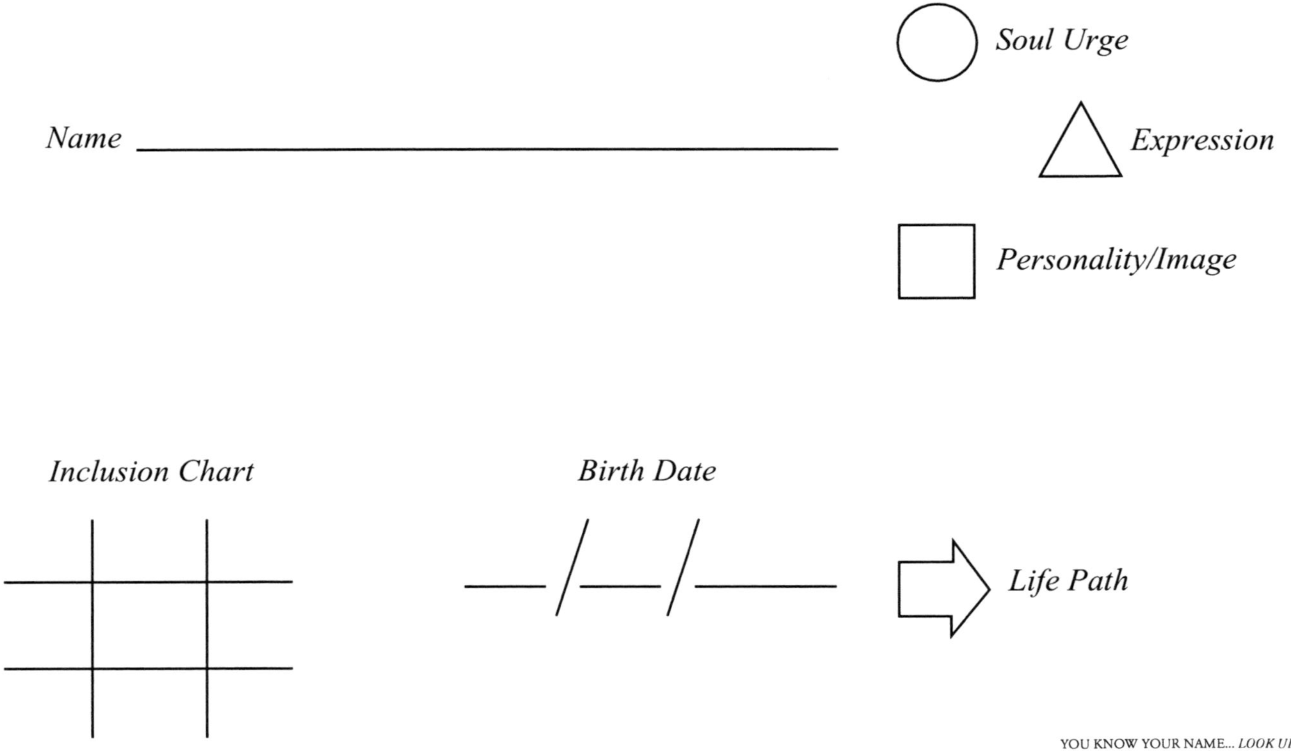

Name _____

⬤ Soul Urge

△ Expression

☐ Personality/Image

Inclusion Chart

Birth Date ___ / ___ / ___

⬇ Life Path

Name _____

○ Soul Urge

△ Expression

☐ Personality/Image

Inclusion Chart

Birth Date ___/___/___

⬇ Life Path

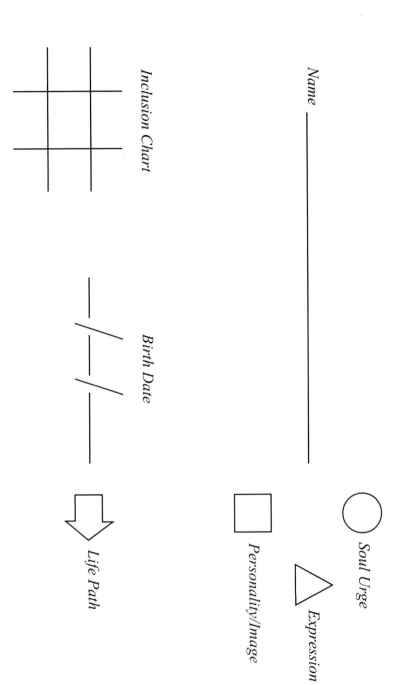

Name _____

◯ Soul Urge

△ Expression

☐ Personality/Image

Inclusion Chart

Birth Date ___/___/___

⬇ Life Path

Name _____

◯ Soul Urge

△ Expression

□ Personality/Image

Inclusion Chart

#

Birth Date ___ / ___ / ___

⬇ Life Path

Name _____

○ Soul Urge

△ Expression

☐ Personality/Image

Inclusion Chart

(grid)

Birth Date ___/___/___

⬇ Life Path

Name _____

○ Soul Urge

△ Expression

□ Personality/Image

Inclusion Chart

#

Birth Date

___ / ___ / ___

⬇ Life Path

Name _____

◯ Soul Urge

△ Expression

☐ Personality/Image

Inclusion Chart

#

Birth Date

___ / ___ / ___

⬇ Life Path

Name _____

◯ Soul Urge

△ Expression

▢ Personality/Image

Inclusion Chart

(tic-tac-toe grid)

Birth Date ___ / ___ / ___

⬇ Life Path

Name

_____

◯ Soul Urge

△ Expression

▢ Personality/Image

Inclusion Chart

Birth Date

___ / ___ / ___

⬇ Life Path

Name _____

◯ Soul Urge

△ Expression

☐ Personality/Image

Inclusion Chart

(grid)

Birth Date — / — / —

⬇ Life Path

Name _____

◯ Soul Urge

△ Expression

☐ Personality/Image

Inclusion Chart

⊞

Birth Date

___ / ___ / ___

⬇ Life Path

Michael John Fierro

ACKNOWLEDGEMENTS

My deepest gratitude to Celeste and Gregg Hinlicky for their work in the editing, layout, and most importantly, the publishing of this book.

I also wish to acknowledge my sister Debra for introducing me to numerology, as well as sharing her personal notebooks on the subject.

To book a session with Michael or to schedule him for a lecture,
send an e-mail to: numerologist_michaelfierro@gmail.com.

Please include an e-mail address and your phone number for contact.

Breinigsville, PA USA
23 August 2010

244011BV00001B/35/P